T0312327

Cambridge Elements ≡

Elements in Decision Theory and Philosophy
edited by
Martin Peterson
Texas A&M University

THE HISTORY AND METHODOLOGY OF EXPECTED UTILITY

Ivan Moscati
University of Insubria
Baffi Carefin, Bocconi University
CPNSS, London School of Economics

CAMBRIDGE
UNIVERSITY PRESS

Shaftesbury Road, Cambridge CB2 8EA, United Kingdom

One Liberty Plaza, 20th Floor, New York, NY 10006, USA

477 Williamstown Road, Port Melbourne, VIC 3207, Australia

314–321, 3rd Floor, Plot 3, Splendor Forum, Jasola District Centre, New Delhi – 110025, India

103 Penang Road, #05–06/07, Visioncrest Commercial, Singapore 238467

Cambridge University Press is part of Cambridge University Press & Assessment, a department of the University of Cambridge.

We share the University's mission to contribute to society through the pursuit of education, learning and research at the highest international levels of excellence.

www.cambridge.org
Information on this title: www.cambridge.org/9781009198264

DOI: 10.1017/9781009198295

First published 2023

A catalogue record for this publication is available from the British Library.

ISBN 978-1-009-19826-4 Paperback
ISSN 2517-4827 (online)
ISSN 2517-4819 (print)

The History and Methodology of Expected Utility

Elements in Decision Theory and Philosophy

DOI: 10.1017/9781009198295
First published online: August 2023

Ivan Moscati
University of Insubria
Baffi Carefin, Bocconi University
CPNSS, London School of Economics

Author for correspondence: Ivan Moscati, ivan.moscati@uninsubria.it

Abstract: This Element offers an accessible but technically detailed review of expected utility theory (EU), which is a model of individual decision-making under uncertainty that is central to both economics and philosophy. The approach of this Element falls between the history of ideas and economic methodology. At the historical level, EU is reviewed by following its conceptual evolution from its original formulation in the eighteenth century through its transformations and extensions in the mid-twentieth century to its more recent supersession by post-EU theories such as prospect theory. In reconstructing the history of EU, the Element focuses on the methodological issues that have accompanied its evolution, such as whether the utility function and the other components of EU correspond to actual mental entities. On many of these issues, no consensus has yet been reached, and in this Element the author offers his view on them.

Keywords: expected utility theory, history of expected utility, methodology of expected utility, risk and uncertainty, prospect theory

ISBNs: 9781009198264 (PB), 9781009198295 (OC)
ISSNs: 2517-4827 (online), 2517-4819 (print)

Contents

1 Introduction

Expected utility theory is a model for the analysis of individual decision-making in situations of risk or uncertainty. These are situations where the outcome of a course of action depends on whether some event occurs. For instance, the outcome of the decision to buy a lottery ticket depends on whether the purchased ticket is drawn, and the outcome of the decision to undergo surgery depends on whether the operation goes well.

In order to state expected utility theory (henceforth EU) with sufficient precision, we need some notation. Assume that N uncertain events E_i are possible, with $i = 1, \ldots, N$, and that they are mutually exclusive (no more than one event can occur at the same time) and jointly exhaustive (at least one of the events must occur). A course of actions yielding outcome x_1 if event E_1 occurs, outcome x_2 if event E_2 occurs, and so on can be represented as $[x_1, E_1; \, x_2, E_2; \ldots; \, x_N, E_N]$. For instance, the lottery-ticket situation can be modeled by stating that there are two possible events: "the purchased ticket is drawn" (event E_1) and "the purchased ticket is not drawn" (event E_2). If event E_1 occurs, the decision maker wins a vacation in Greece and is even reimbursed for the lottery ticket (outcome x_1); if event E_2 occurs, the decision maker loses the five euros he paid for the ticket (outcome x_2).

Assume also that, for each event E_i, it is possible to identify the probability $p(E_i)$ that the event occurs. Such probability can be an "objective" probability that the decision maker knows. For instance, if there are 10,000 lottery tickets, the objective probability that the purchased ticket is drawn is 1 in 10,000, or 0.0001. In this case, decision theorists talk of decision-making "under risk." If objective probabilities are not available or are not known by the decision maker, decision theorists talk of decision-making "under uncertainty." In this case, $p(E_i)$ can be seen as a "subjective" probability expressing the decision maker's degree of belief that event E_i will occur. For instance, if the decision maker believes that the surgery goes well nine times out of ten, the subjective probability $p(E_i)$ is 0.9.[1]

Finally, suppose that there exists a real-valued function $u(\cdot)$ that assigns a number $u(x_i)$ to each outcome x_i. For instance, $u(holiday\ in\ Greece) = 60,000$ and $u(-5\ Euros) = -7$. This function is called a "utility function" and, as we will discuss, the meaning of the numbers $u(x_i)$ is a controversial issue.

---

[1] From a philosophical perspective, and in particular in the light of the enormous literature generated by Lewis's ([1980] 1987) paper on chance and credence, the distinction between "objective" and "subjective" probability used in decision theory may appear simplistic. However, as will become clear in the following sections, it is sufficient for the purposes of this Element.

For the moment, however, it suffices to say that EU states that the value a decision maker assigns to a course of action $[x_1, E_1; \ldots; x_N, E_N]$ is expressed by its "expected utility" – in other words, by the average of the utility values $u(x_i)$, each weighted by its probability $p(E_i)$; that is, the value of a course of action is expressed by $\sum_{i=1}^{N} u(x_i)p(E_i)$. In order to lighten the notation, when the indexing of variables is not needed, I shall write this formula as just $\sum u(x_i)p(E_i)$.

In our example, the expected utility of the course of action "buy the lottery ticket" is $60,000 \times \frac{1}{10,000} + (-7) \times \frac{9,999}{10,000}$, which is around -1.

1.1 The Two Faces of EU: Normative and Descriptive

Expected utility theory has a double character: It is both "normative" and "descriptive." As a normative theory, EU states what a sensible or, as economists and philosophers tend to say, a "rational" decision maker ought to do: select the course of action associated with the highest expected utility. For instance, if the expected utility attached to the course of action "don't buy the lottery ticket" is higher than the expected utility attached to the course of action "buy the ticket," the decision maker ought not buy the ticket. Intended as a descriptive theory, EU aims at describing what actual decision makers do, even if their behavior might not appear rational.

In principle, the two faces of EU are disconnected, in the sense that EU could be normatively valid but descriptively invalid. Thus, the decision maker may agree that it is not sensible for him to buy the lottery ticket but then, for some reason, he might buy it anyway.[2] However, as we will see, the history of EU shows that the normative and descriptive dimensions of the theory are strictly interrelated.

1.2 EU in Economics and Philosophy

EU for decision-making under risk was originally advanced by Daniel Bernoulli ([1738] 1982) in the eighteenth century but entered economics much later, in the 1870s. Since then, EU has undergone changing fortunes in the discipline. Between the 1870s and 1910s, most economists accepted it, although with some reservations. In the 1920s and 1930s, in the context of the so-called ordinal turn in utility analysis, further criticisms against the theory were raised, and by the early 1940s the supporters of EU in economics were few. The fortunes of EU began to recover in the mid-1940s, when John von Neumann and Oskar

---

[2] In order to maintain gender equilibrium in the use of third-person singular personal pronouns without impairing the readability of the text, I shall use masculine pronouns in odd sections and feminine pronouns in even sections.

Morgenstern ([1944] 1953) advanced a novel, preference-based version of the theory.

In the von Neumann–Morgenstern version, and with the extension to decision-making under uncertainty provided by Leonard Jimmie Savage ([1954] 1972), EU became the dominant economic model of individual decision-making under risk and uncertainty, a position that it retained at least until the 1990s.

Beginning in the 1970s, the accumulation of robust experimental evidence against EU prompted decision theorists to advance a number of models alternative to EU, such as prospect theory (Kahneman & Tversky 1979; Tversky & Kahneman 1992). However, none of these alternative models has yet achieved the level of consensus that EU once enjoyed. For this reason, and also thanks to its simplicity and adaptability, EU remains the primary model in numerous areas of economics dealing with decisions under risk or uncertainty, such as finance, the theory of asymmetric information, and game theory.

Expected utility theory has also played an important role in philosophy. Since the mid-1950s, EU has been used as a normative theory of rational choice (Davidson, McKinsey, & Suppes 1955). With some simplification, we may say that in philosophy EU has maintained this normative status until the present. Philosophers have paid relatively little attention to the non-EU models advanced in the last forty years or so, and this is primarily because they do not perceive them as normatively valid (for a discussion, see Buchak 2013; Okasha 2016; Bradley 2017).

In the 1970s, David Lewis (1974) and other philosophers began to attach a further meaning to EU, namely that it offers a formalized version of the common-sense, or folk-psychological, understanding of decision-making. According to this interpretation, common sense suggests that our decisions result from the combination of our desires and beliefs. Expected utility theory would capture desires through the utility function $u(x)$ and beliefs through the probability function $p(E)$, and it would indicate a simple way to combine them, via the formula $\sum u(x_i)p(E_i)$. However, as we will discuss, this interpretation is debatable. In particular, it is controversial whether the utility function $u(x)$ can be actually interpreted as capturing desires and whether the summations and multiplications needed to calculate the value $\sum u(x_i)p(E_i)$ are really simple.

1.3 This Element

In this Element, I offer an accessible but technically detailed review of EU. My approach falls between the history of ideas and economic methodology. At the historical level, I review EU by following its conceptual evolution from its original formulation in the eighteenth century through its transformations and extensions in the mid-twentieth century to more recent supersession by post-EU theories such as prospect theory. In reconstructing the history of EU, I focus on the methodological issues that have accompanied its evolution: Is EU descriptively and/or normatively valid? Can the utility function featured in EU be interpreted as expressing how intensely a decision maker desires an outcome? More generally, do the utility function and the other components of EU correspond to entities that actually exist in the minds of decision makers, or are they best understood as fictional constructs that may lack any mental reference? On many of these issues, no consensus has yet been reached, and in this Element I offer my view on them.

In Section 2, I first reconstruct how EU originated in the discussions that some mathematicians of the late seventeenth and early eighteenth centuries had about the likelihood of certain aleatory events occurring in betting; I then illustrate Bernoulli's version of EU and discuss its explanatory structure from a methodological viewpoint. In Section 3, I explain why most economists accepted Bernoulli's EU between the 1870s and 1910s and how the "ordinal turn" in utility analysis, which was completed by the late 1930s, led to a generalized rejection of the theory. Section 4 presents von Neumann and Morgenstern's novel, preference-based version of EU. In Section 5, I discuss a number of theoretical and methodological issues related to von Neumann and Morgenstern's EU, such as its relationship with Bernoulli's EU, its descriptive and normative validity, including a discussion of the "Allais paradox," and the appropriate interpretation of the utility function $\tilde{u}(x)$ featured in von Neumann and Morgenstern's EU. In Section 6, I move to Savage's extension of EU to situations of uncertainty; among other things, I discuss the descriptive and normative validity of Savage's EU, including an illustration of the "Ellsberg paradox," and the theoretical status of the utility function $\tilde{u}(x)$ and the probability measure $p(E)$ featured in Savage's theory. Finally, Section 7 presents a quick overview of the theories that go beyond EU and have been advanced since the mid-1970s. I am convinced that certain features of EU become fully clear only when it is contrasted with theories alternative to it. In particular, I focus on prospect theory, which arguably is the most influential of the post-EU theories, and compare the ways in which EU and prospect theory model risk attitudes; at the methodological level, I argue that, contrary to what its advocates typically claim, prospect theory is not psychologically more realistic than EU and, like EU, is best understood as an "as-if" model of decision-making.

A few final remarks about the scope and features of the present Element are in order. First, although technically detailed, my review of EU attempts to be mathematically accessible to any student of economics and philosophy. Readers seeking a mathematically more advanced presentation of EU may consult other works, such as Kreps (1988) or Gilboa (2009). Second, the overview of the post-EU theories I offer in Section 7 is extremely limited. Several comprehensive works reviewing this literature are available: Schoemaker (1982), Starmer (2000), Wakker (2010), Gilboa and Marinacci (2013), and Lipman and Pesendorfer (2013) focus on the economic literature, while Peterson (2017) and Steele and Stefánsson (2020) concentrate on the philosophical literature. Finally, some parts of this Element draw on related work of mine: The more historical parts draw on Moscati (2016) and Moscati (2018), and the more methodological sections are based on Moscati (in press).

2 Bernoulli's EU

2.1 A New Field of Study

The scientific disciplines that we today call probability theory and decision theory came into being as a single field of study around 1650, when the French mathematicians Blaise Pascal and Pierre de Fermat, as well as the Dutch mathematician and astronomer Christiaan Huygens, used a principled approach to solve issues related to gaming and betting that had been occasionally discussed since the late fifteenth century. These issues deal with the likelihood of certain aleatory events related to dice throwing or coin tossing, the fair price to pay in order to participate in such events, and the so-called problem of points, which concerns the equitable division of a monetary prize in a game of chance interrupted before completion.

The new field of study displayed contrasting dimensions that have accompanied its evolution, and later the evolution of probability theory and decision theory, until the present. First, the idea of probability was dual from its very emergence. As the historian Ian Hacking (1975, 1) stressed, the probability notion was originally connected, on the one hand, "with the degree of belief warranted by evidence" and, on the other, "with the tendency, displayed by some chance devices, to produce stable relative frequencies."

The analysis of decisions was also dual from the start, as it was both normative and descriptive. For early decision theorists, the normative dimension was the dominant one, and their analysis mostly concerned the maximum price that people of good sense should pay to participate in certain games of chance, or the equitable division of money in the problem of points. However, early decision theorists also aimed at describing what people actually do and therefore tested the normative recommendations obtained by mathematical reasoning against introspective psychological evidence, or against the ordinary behavior of competent individuals, such as merchants or skilled players of games of chance.

2.2 Expected Payoff

One common tenet of the theories put forward by Pascal, Fermat, and Huygens was the identification of what today we call "mathematical expectation," "expected value," or "expected payoff" as the parameter indicating the fair price of a monetary gamble. Using the notation introduced in Section 1, the expected payoff of a course of action $[x_1, E_1; \ldots; x_N, E_N]$ that yields monetary payoff x_i if event E_i occurs is given by $\sum x_i p(E_i)$. For brevity, I call the "expected-payoff hypothesis" the tenet that the fair price of a monetary gamble corresponds to its expected payoff.

The most explicit supporter of this hypothesis was Huygens, whose book *De ratiociniis in ludo aleae* (*On Calculation in Games of Chance*, 1657) was the first published treatise in the new field of study. To illustrate the hypothesis, Huygens considered a game in which an individual hides three shillings in one hand and seven shillings in the other, while another individual chooses one of the hands. For Huygens, to the latter individual this gamble is worth $\frac{1}{2} \times 3 + \frac{1}{2} \times 7 = 5$ shillings. More generally, Huygens stated that "if I have the same chance to get a or b [where a and b are amounts of money], the game is worth to me as much as $\frac{a+b}{2}$" (Huygens [1657] 1920, 62–63).

During the period 1660–1710, the expected-payoff hypothesis was accepted by most scholars working in the field, including, among others, two members of the Bernoulli family of Swiss mathematicians, Jakob Bernoulli and his nephew Nicolaus Bernoulli. In his influential book *Ars conjectandi* (*The Art of Conjecturing*, completed in 1705 but published posthumously in 1713), Jakob argued that the expected-payoff hypothesis is "the fundamental principle of the whole art [of conjecturing]" (Bernoulli [1713] 2006, 134). In his doctoral dissertation *De usu artis conjectandi in iure* (*On the Use of the Art of Conjecturing in Law*, 1709), Nicolaus applied probability and decision theory to a series of practical issues, ranging from insurance theory to life expectancy. Following Huygens and his uncle Jakob, Nicolaus also maintained that mathematical expectation is the fundamental parameter on which the art of conjecturing should be based (Bernoulli [1709] 1975, 290–291). However, it was Nicolaus himself who, some years later, conceived a game situation that contradicted the expected-payoff hypothesis.

2.3 Nicolaus Bernoulli's Game and Moral Impossibility

In a letter to the French mathematician Pierre Rémond de Montmort dated September 9, 1713 (see Spiess 1975, 557), Nicolaus Bernoulli imagined a game of dice in which individual A pays one *écu* (a French coin used before the Revolution of 1789) to individual B if, by rolling a die, B obtains a six on the first throw, two *écus* if B obtains a six on the second throw, four *écus* if B obtains a six on the third throw, and so on. The expected payoff of this game is $\left(1 \times \frac{1}{6}\right) + \left(2 \times \frac{5}{36}\right) + \left(4 \times \frac{25}{216}\right) + \ldots$, that is, $\sum_{i=0}^{\infty} 2^i \frac{5^i}{6^{i+1}}$, which is a positive infinite number. Therefore, according to the expected-payoff hypothesis, B ought to pay an infinite amount of money to participate in this game. This appeared to Nicolaus not only descriptively implausible but also normatively wrong.

In further correspondence with de Montmort (Spiess 1975, 558–560), Nicolaus proposed to overcome the problem by introducing some "moral," that is, psychological, element into the purely mathematical expected-payoff formula. In particular, Nicolaus made use of the notion of "morally impossible" (*moraliter impossibile*) events put forward by his uncle Jakob in *Ars conjectandi* (Bernoulli [1713] 2006, 316). Jakob had argued that people of good sense consider events with a very small probability as impossible and therefore treat them as if the probability of these events were zero. Nicolaus applied this idea to his dice game and argued that people are willing to pay only a limited amount of money to participate in it because they consider the events associated with high gains as morally impossible.

Considered from a contemporary viewpoint, Jakob's and Nicolaus's idea that individuals may attach to an event a moral weight that is different from its objective probability has some common traits with the idea of "probability weighting" that will be discussed in Section 7 as a key feature of prospect theory.

2.4 Cramer's Game and Moral Value

Some years later, in 1728, Nicolaus resumed the discussion about the game and its conflict with the expected-payoff hypothesis in correspondence with Gabriel Cramer, another eminent Swiss mathematician. In a letter to Nicolaus dated May 21, 1728 (Spiess 1975, 560–561), Cramer put forward a simplified version of the game in which a coin rather than a die was used. In Cramer's setting, A pays one *écu* to B if, by tossing a coin, B obtains tails on the first throw, two *écus* if B obtains tails on the second throw, four *écus* if B obtains tails on the third throw, and so on. Cramer calculated that the expected payoff of this coin game is $\left(1 \times \frac{1}{2}\right) + \left(2 \times \frac{1}{4}\right) + \left(4 \times \frac{1}{8}\right) + \ldots = \frac{1}{2} + \frac{1}{2} + \frac{1}{2} + \ldots$, that is, infinite, just like the expected payoff of Nicolaus's game. It is Cramer's coin game, and not Nicolaus's dice game, that was later labeled the "St. Petersburg game" (see Section 2.6.2).

2.4.1 Moral Value

Cramer agreed with Nicolaus that "no person of good sense" (*de bon sens*) (Spiess 1975, 560) would be willing to pay an infinite amount of money to participate in games such as those he and Nicolaus had conceived of. In order to solve the problem, Cramer also introduced a "moral," meaning a psychological, element in the expected-payoff formula. But while Nicolaus focused on morally impossible events, that is, on the psychological evaluation of probabilities, Cramer concentrated on "moral values," that is, on the psychological evaluation of money.

In his letter to Nicolaus, Cramer argued that the reason for the discrepancy between the expected-payoff hypothesis and the behavior of reasonable people stems from the fact that "mathematicians evaluate money in proportion to its quantity while people of good sense evaluate money in proportion to the use they can make of it" (560). Cramer called people's evaluation of money the *"moral value"* (*valeur morale*) of money.

Cramer submitted two distinct hypotheses about the moral value of money. First, people may consider all amounts of money above a certain level as equivalent. For instance, Cramer suggested, if an individual considers all amounts of money above $2^{24} = 16,777,216$ *écus* as equivalent, the price she is willing to pay to participate in the St. Petersburg game is not infinite, and more precisely is around 13 *écus*. Second, Cramer observed that "100 million yield more satisfaction than 10 million, but not 10 times as much" (Spiess 1975, 561); in other words, the moral value of money increases less than proportionally to the increase of money. For Cramer, a possible way of capturing this circumstance is to assume that the moral value of a sum of money x is given by its square root $\sqrt{x}$. Under this latter assumption, Cramer continued, the "moral expectation" (*esperance morale*) of the coin game is finite (as opposed to its infinite mathematical expectation), and the price a person of good sense ought to pay for the game is less than three *écus*.

2.4.2 Priority Issues

Considered from a contemporary standpoint, Cramer's two hypotheses are already instantiations of EU. What Cramer called the moral value of money is akin to the utility of money $u(x)$, and both of his hypotheses state that the value of the coin game is given by $\sum u(x_i)p(E_i)$. In the first hypothesis $u(x_i) = x_i$ for all $x_i \leq 2^{24}$, and $u(x_i) = 2^{24}$ for all $x_i > 2^{24}$, while in the second hypothesis $u(x_i) = \sqrt{x_i}$ for all x_i. Nonetheless, I think that the standard practice of associating the birth of EU with Daniel Bernoulli (introduced in Section 2.5) is legitimate, and this is for various reasons.

First, as we will see in a moment, Bernoulli was not aware of Cramer's hypotheses when he proposed his own version of EU. Second, Bernoulli's arguments in favor of EU are much more extended and systematic than the arguments cursorily suggested by Cramer in his letter to Nicolaus. Third, the two theories are similar but not identical, and in particular Cramer did not take into account the initial wealth of decision makers. Finally, Bernoulli was the first to put his ideas into print, which he did in 1738.

2.5 Enter Daniel

In August 1728, Nicolaus involved in the discussion about games with an infinite mathematical payoff his cousin Daniel Bernoulli (1700–82), a mathematician and a physicist who at that time held a professorship at the Academy of Sciences in St. Petersburg, Russia. In a letter to Daniel dated August 27, 1728, Nicolaus described the game in the simplified, coin version proposed by Cramer; mentioned that Cramer had proposed a solution but did not illustrate what this solution was; and asked for Daniel's opinion on the issue. Initially, Daniel did not fully understand the problem, but after some time and some further exchange with Nicolaus, he worked out his own theory and outlined it in a paper that he sent to Nicolaus on July 4, 1731. Based on this paper, which has been recently rediscovered (see Mata & Nagel 2023), Daniel presented his theory at the St. Petersburg Academy in March 1732.

Nicolaus reacted to Daniel's paper only later, on April 5, 1732. He was not convinced by Daniel's theory and defended his own solution based on neglecting morally impossible events. Nicolaus also noted the similarity between Daniel's theory and the theory Cramer had advanced in his letter of May 1728 and attached a copy of Cramer's letter to his reply to Daniel. Thus, Daniel became aware of Cramer's theory only after presenting his paper at the St. Petersburg Academy in March 1732.

Daniel's paper was published much later, in 1738, with the title *Specimen theoriae novae de mensura sortis* ("Exposition of a New Theory on the Measurement of Risk") in the proceedings of the St. Petersburg Academy (Bernoulli [1738] 1982; English translation: Bernoulli [1738] 1954).[3] The published version of the essay is not significantly different from the original one Daniel drafted in 1731. Apparently, the name "St. Petersburg game," which is what Cramer's coin game is usually called, originates in the fact that the game was discussed in print for the first time in the proceedings of the St. Petersburg Academy, that is, in Daniel's article.

2.6 Daniel Bernoulli's *emolumentum medium*

Daniel Bernoulli presented his theory as "new" in explicit opposition to the then dominant theory, the expected-payoff hypothesis. For Daniel, the fundamental drawback of the expected-payoff hypothesis is that it rules out any

---

[3] I find the English translation of Bernoulli's essay problematic in many respects and therefore in the following quotations I have often modified it.

personal element in the evaluation of risky alternatives: "It is clear that all men cannot apply the same rule to measure risk and, that, therefore, the rule mentioned in §1 [the expected-payoff principle] should be rejected" (Bernoulli [1738] 1954, 24). To support his point, Daniel considered how a poor man and a rich man evaluate a gamble that yields with equal probability either nothing or 20,000 ducats, which was then a significant amount of money. According to the expected-payoff hypothesis, both should evaluate the gamble at 10,000 ducats, and the poor would be mistaken in selling the gamble to the rich for 9,000 ducats. For Daniel, however, that trade could be advisable for both: The poor could be better off by having 9,000 ducats for sure rather than risk remaining poor, and the rich could afford the risk of losing 9,000 ducats for an even chance of getting 20,000.

For Daniel, in order to develop a sound theory of the evaluation of risky alternatives it is necessary to distinguish between the monetary value of a thing, which he called its "price" (*pretium*), and its subjective value, which Daniel did not call utility, or *valeur morale*, but *emolumentum*, that is, advantage or benefit. For him, the benefit rather than the price should be taken into account in the evaluation of risk: "The price of a thing depends only on the thing itself and is the same for everyone; its benefit (*emolumentum*) depends on the condition of the person. ... No valid measurement of risk can be obtained, unless we consider the benefit that any given person obtains from a certain [monetary] gain" (24).

Daniel then stated his theory: The traditional principle of mathematical expectation should be preserved, but it should be applied to the mathematical expectation of the benefit rather than the mathematical expectation of money:

> By multiplying each expected benefit by the number of cases in which it can occur, and dividing the sum of these products by the total number of possible cases, an average benefit (*emolumentum medium*) will be obtained. The gain corresponding to this benefit will be equal to the value of the risk alternative in question. (24)

Daniel's next step is to identify a plausible relationship between an amount of money x and the benefit y associated with it. He argues that, at least in general, the increase of benefit dy that a person with wealth a obtains from an increase dx of her wealth is directly proportional to dx and inversely proportional to a. This implies that the total benefit y that a person with initial wealth a gets from a monetary gain x is given by the natural logarithm of $(a + x)$, that is, $y = \log(a + x)$. For Daniel, the logarithmic form of the benefit function is equal for every individual. What distinguishes different individuals is only that they have different initial amounts of wealth.

2.6.1 Some Implications

Daniel draws a number of implications from his hypothesis. First, whatever the individual's initial wealth, if she bets on what today we call an "actuarially fair" gamble, that is, on a gamble whose price is equal to its monetary mathematical expectation, the individual suffers an expected loss. If the gamble is less than actuarially fair, that is, if it costs more than its monetary mathematical expectation, the expected loss is clearly higher.

For instance, if a person has an initial wealth of 100 ducats and bets 50 ducats on an actuarially fair game that pays 0 ducats or 100 ducats with equal probability, the expected benefit is $\frac{1}{2}\log(100 - 50) + \frac{1}{2}\log(100 - 50 + 100)$, which is less than the benefit she has if she does not bet, that is, $\log(100)$. Therefore, Daniel concludes, it is not advisable to bet, not only if a bet is less than actuarially fair, as bets typically are, but even if a bet is fair. He stresses that this conclusion does not depend on the assumption that the benefit function is logarithmic but only on the assumption that the function is concave ("*ex concavitate curvae*," 29), that is, using a later terminology, from the assumption that the marginal benefit of money is diminishing (see Section 3).

Second, Daniel investigates the following question: If it is unwise to pay the expected monetary payoff of a gamble to participate in it, what is the maximum price h that a person of good sense with initial wealth a should pay? For a simple gamble yielding a net gain k with probability $\frac{1}{2}$, and a loss h, equal to its price, with probability $\frac{1}{2}$, it should be that $\frac{1}{2}\log(a - h) + \frac{1}{2}\log(a + k) = \log(a)$, that is, $h = \frac{ak}{a+k}$. This value, stresses Daniel, is less than the expected monetary payoff of the gamble. This confirms the first conclusion, namely that, whatever the individual's initial wealth, she ought not to bet on gambles whose price is equal or higher than their expected payoff.

Third, Daniel applies his theory to insurance. Caius, a St. Petersburg merchant, has an initial wealth of a rubles and expects a ship from Amsterdam carrying commodities worth 10,000 rubles. He knows that there is a probability $\frac{5}{100}$ that the ship sinks, but for 800 rubles he can buy from Sempronius an insurance policy that fully repays him in case of a shipwreck. Daniel investigates how much initial wealth Caius should possess in order for it to be sensible for him to refrain from buying the insurance and what initial wealth β Sempronius should possess in order for it to be sensible for him to insure Caius.

Concerning Caius, he should possess an initial wealth a such that the expected benefit associated with the course of action "don't buy the insurance," that is, $\frac{95}{100}\log(a + 10{,}000) + \frac{5}{100}\log(a)$, is at least as large as the expected benefit associated with the course of action "buy the insurance," that is,

$\log(\alpha + 10{,}000 - 800)$. Daniel shows that Caius should possess an initial wealth of at least 5,043 rubles.

Moving to Sempronius, he should possess an initial wealth β such that the expected benefit associated with the course of action "insure Caius," that is, $\frac{95}{100}\log(\beta + 800) + \frac{5}{100}\log(\beta + 800 - 10{,}000)$, is at least as large as the expected benefit associated with the course of action "don't insure Caius," that is, $\log(\beta)$. It turns out that Sempronius's initial wealth β should be at least 14,243 rubles. Daniel also notes that, if the price of the insurance were equal to the monetary expected payoff of the "insurance game," that is, $\frac{5}{100}10{,}000 + \frac{95}{100}0 = 500$, it would not be advisable for Sempronius, however rich he might be, to insure Caius. This result further confirms the first two implications of the theory.

2.6.2 St. Petersburg Game

Finally, and only at the end of his paper, Daniel applies his theory to games with an infinite monetary payoff like those imagined by his cousin Nicolaus and by Cramer. In particular, Daniel focuses on Cramer's version of the game. In Daniel's rendering of the story, the player is named Paul, the currency at stake is the ducat, and Paul's initial wealth is equal to α ducats. According to Daniel's theory, for Paul the value of the St. Petersburg game is given by $\frac{1}{2}\log(\alpha + 1) + \frac{1}{4}\log(\alpha + 2) + \frac{1}{8}\log(\alpha + 4) + \ldots$ Daniel finds that, if $\alpha = 0$, the game is worth to Paul 2 ducats; if $\alpha = 10$, the game is worth around 3 ducats; and if $\alpha = 1{,}000$, the game is worth around 6 ducats, that is, incomparably less than what is suggested by the expected-payoff hypothesis.

In the final part of his paper, Daniel reproduces the letter that Cramer had sent to Nicolaus in 1728 and that Nicolaus had forwarded to him in 1732. Daniel acknowledged that Cramer had advanced a similar theory before him but also stressed that he had presented his hypothesis at the St. Petersburg Academy before becoming aware of Cramer's theory. Daniel added that Cramer's and his own approaches were so similar that it seemed to him "miraculous that we independently reached such close agreement on this sort of subject" (33). Notably, in his paper Daniel did not mention Nicolaus's theory based on the idea of neglecting morally impossible events.

2.7 Bernoulli's EU: Discussion

After illustrating in some detail Daniel Bernoulli's theory, we can now discuss it from a methodological viewpoint.

2.7.1 Explanatory Structure

A first feature to be considered is the explanatory structure of Bernoulli's EU, which will be later contrasted with the explanatory structure of von Neumann and Morgenstern's EU. To anticipate the key point, while Bernoulli attempts to explain how individuals evaluate, or should evaluate, risky options as the effect of other factors, and notably as the result of how individuals evaluate riskless money, von Neumann and Morgenstern take the decision maker's preferences between risky options as given and are not interested in explaining them.

Focusing now on Bernoulli, his explanation of people's behavior under conditions of risk relies on three factors: (1) the probabilities of the various possible events; (2) the benefit that people attach to money; and (3) the way these two elements are combined, that is, by the multiplications and summations that yield the average benefit. We consider in sequence each of these factors.

2.7.2 Objective Probabilities

Concerning probabilities, Daniel focuses on the case of so-called objective probabilities (see Section 1) that the decision maker is supposed to know. As already discussed, his cousin Nicolaus suggested that decision makers attach a subjective weight to some objective probabilities, namely a subjective weight of zero to small objective probabilities. Daniel did not subscribe to this assumption.

2.7.3 Benefit of Money

Concerning the benefit that individuals attach to money, this is either the benefit $\log(\alpha)$ attached to the individual's initial wealth if she decides not to participate in the gamble or, if she participates in the gamble, the benefit $\log(\alpha + x)$ attached to her final wealth, after one of the N possible events is realized, that is, after the uncertainty associated with the gamble is resolved. In both cases, and this is the important point, the benefit at issue is the benefit of money under conditions of certainty, not risk. This means that Bernoulli explains what people prefer, or should prefer, under conditions of risk on the basis of what people prefer, or should prefer, under conditions of certainty.

Moreover, and this is another important element of Bernoulli's theory, the benefit attached to riskless money is the *unique* subjective factor that explains people's behavior under risk. This means that in the theory there is no room for other psychological factors, specifically associated with situations of risk, that can be added to the benefit of money in order to explain behavior under risk.

This latter aspect of Bernoulli's theory is evident in the way it accounts for the individual's attitudes toward risk. In his theory, risk attitudes are not a specific and primitive psychological trait of the individual but are fully determined by her attitude toward riskless money. In particular, since Bernoulli assumes that the benefit function is concave, that is, that the marginal benefit of money is diminishing, for him all individuals are, or should be, risk-averse, in the specific sense that they reject, or should reject, actuarially fair gambles (on the definition of risk aversion, see Section 5.2). In other words, in Bernoulli's theory individuals are risk-averse because, *and only because*, the marginal benefit of money is diminishing.

As will be discussed in Section 7, prospect theory introduces further and independent factors that add to the diminishing marginal benefit of money in explaining risk attitudes, such as "loss aversion" or "probability weighting."

2.7.4 Benefit of Money (Continued)

Concerning the benefit that individuals attach to money, two further points are worth mentioning. First, for Bernoulli the logarithmic benefit function is the same for all individuals. So, in a sense, everybody evaluates money in the same way. The only difference between individuals is their initial wealth, and it is this difference that makes them attach different benefits to the same option and therefore allows for trade of options between people. If, in Bernoulli's insurance example, Caius and Sempronius had the same initial wealth there would be no purchase and sale of insurance. It is in order to remark that in contemporary uses of EU it is often assumed that different types of agents have different utility functions for money. In insurance theory, for example, the insurer typically has a linear utility function, while the potential client has a concave utility function. In this case, trade can occur even if the two agents have the same initial wealth: At a price slightly higher than the actuarially fair price, the linear-utility insurer is willing to sell the insurance and the concave-utility client is willing to buy it.

The second point concerns Bernoulli's conception of the status of the benefit a person attaches to money. He appears to believe that the benefit of money and the circumstance that the marginal benefit of money decreases as the person's wealth increases are actually existing features of people's minds. In other words, Bernoulli appears to be a realist or, to use a more recent term, a mentalist about the benefit of money.

2.7.5 Mechanism: Multiply and Add

The third element of Bernoulli's explanation of people's behavior under conditions of risk relates to the mechanism by which the probabilities of possible events and the benefit of money are combined, namely by the series of multiplications and summation that yield the average benefit or, if we identify Bernoulli's benefit with the later notion of utility (see Section 3), the average utility $\sum u(x_i)p(E_i)$.

A first question is whether people, when choosing among risky options, actually perform, and perform correctly, the calculations needed to arrive at the value $\sum u(x_i)p(E_i)$. Casual introspection suggests that this is not the case. Moreover, modern psychological research on numerical skills and cognition (see, e.g., Nuerk, Moeller, & Willmes 2015) shows that normal individuals face significant difficulties dealing with addition and multiplication tasks much simpler than those involved in the calculation of $\sum u(x_i)p(E_i)$. In effect, as will be discussed in Section 5, modern advocates of EU do not claim that individuals actually calculate $\sum u(x_i)p(E_i)$, and interpret the multiply-and-add mechanism featured in EU as an "as-if" mechanism, that is, as a fictional mechanism that does not actually operate in the mind of decision makers.

At any rate, just as Huygens and the other advocates of the expected-payoff hypothesis did not discuss whether people actually perform the calculations needed to arrive at $\sum x_i p(E_i)$, so Bernoulli did not discuss whether people perform calculations needed to arrive at $\sum u(x_i)p(E_i)$. This lack of discussion, I submit, stems from the fact that these early decision theorists were mostly interested in the normative forcefulness of their theories than in their descriptive validity.

2.7.6 Why the Average?

There is, however, another issue that Bernoulli did not address. His theory states that individuals base their decisions on the average of utilities and thus implicitly rules out the possibility that individuals take also into account other elements of the utility distribution, such as its variance. However, is it correct, from a descriptive viewpoint, that individuals discard the variance and other elements of the utility distribution? And, from a normative perspective, would they be legitimate or "rational" in doing so? A simple example suggests that this is far from obvious.

Consider Sempronius again. If he possesses an initial wealth of 14,243 rubles, the expected benefit of the course of action "insure Caius," that is, $\frac{95}{100}\log(15{,}043) + \frac{5}{100}\log(5{,}043)$, is the same as the expected benefit of the course of action "don't insure Caius," that is, $\log(14{,}243)$. Therefore, according to Bernoulli's theory, Sempronius should be indifferent between the two courses of action. However, while in the latter course of action there is no variability in the benefit – it is always $\log(14{,}243)$) – in the former course of action the benefit could be either $\log(15{,}043)$ or $\log(5{,}043)$, that is, the variance of the benefit is larger than zero. One may imagine that Sempronius does not like this variance, possibly because it gives him some disquietude. Thus Sempronius might still prefer not to insure Caius at 800 rubles, or he might ask Caius for an extra 50 rubles as compensation for that disquietude. From a descriptive viewpoint, all this seems plausible. And even from a normative perspective, it seems difficult to argue that Sempronius's disquietude is "irrational."

Bernoulli did not discuss why focusing on the expected benefit only, and so discarding the variance and other elements of the utility distribution, is an appropriate approach. He was happy to provide an extension of the expected-payoff hypothesis that was as close as possible to that hypothesis but capable of explaining phenomena that the then dominant theory was not able to account for, such as the insurance practices of merchants and the circumstance that people are not willing to pay an infinite amount of money to participate in the St. Petersburg game.

3 Fortunes and Misfortunes of Bernoulli's EU

During the eighteenth and nineteenth centuries, Bernoulli's theory was discussed by a number of philosophers and mathematicians and notably by the French polymath Pierre-Simon Laplace (1812, 441–454), who referred to it as the theory of moral expectation (*espérance morale*). The theory entered economic thought only much later, in the 1870s, when the price of a commodity began to be seen as depending on the utility that it has for the individuals in the economy.

3.1 Early Utility Theory and Its Problems

Before 1870, most economists, including Adam Smith, David Ricardo, and Karl Marx, explained prices by using the so-called labor theory of value, according to which the price of a commodity is determined by the quantity of labor needed to produce it. Bernoulli's account of the value of risky prospects is unrelated to the quantity of labor needed to produce them, and this can explain why the economists of the period 1770–1870 ignored it.

In the early 1870s, William Stanley Jevons (1871), Carl Menger ([1871] 1981), and Léon Walras ([1874] 1954) independently put forward a different explanation of exchange value. They argued that the price of a commodity depends on its utility, and more specifically, on its marginal utility. This is the additional utility associated with an individual's consumption of an additional unit of the commodity. In particular, the three economists assumed that individuals attempt to maximize the utility they obtain from commodities and that the marginal utility of each commodity diminishes as the individual consumes a larger quantity of it. On the basis of these assumptions, Jevons, Menger, and Walras were able to construct comprehensive theories of demand, supply, and market equilibrium.

During the last quarter of the nineteenth century, their theories were refined and extended by a second generation of marginal-utility theorists, and by around 1900 most economists accepted the marginal utility approach to economic analysis. However, utility theory was far from flawless. Here, we call attention to two important problematic aspects.

First, as critics have pointed out since the emergence of utility theory (see, e.g., Cairnes 1872), utility cannot be observed and measured in a straightforward way; this circumstance, in turn, would undermine the utility-based explanation of prices. In fact, critics argued, if marginal utility cannot be measured, how do we know that a utility-based explanation of price, such as, "The price of this commodity is 20 shillings *because* its marginal utility is 2," is correct?

The second problem concerned the very definition of utility. Menger identified utility with what satisfies a physiological need. Jevons associated it with the satisfaction of low-level pleasures, which can go beyond physiological needs. Walras's notion is even broader, and for him utility is associated with the satisfaction of pleasures and desires of any type, for example the pleasure of admiring a painting. However, critics of utility theory, such as Schmoller (1883), argued that the broadening of the definition of utility had not modified its fundamental selfish character: The needs, pleasures, or desires that, according to utility theorists, the individual seeks to maximize are his own needs, pleasures, and desires. According to critics, this portrayal of human beings as purely egoistic subjects who are focused only on their well-being at the expense of any social, ethical, or religious motivations is unrealistic and misleading.

The early utility theorists offered a variety of possible solutions to these problems, but it is fair to say that by 1900 they were still open (for a discussion, see Moscati 2018).

3.2 Bernoulli's Theory and Early Utility Analysis

Returning to Bernoulli, his theory fitted nicely in the marginal-utility framework. Jevons and other utility theorists such as Alfred Marshall reinterpreted Bernoulli's notion of *emolumentum* and Cramer's notion of *valeur morale* as equivalent to the notion of utility; Bernoulli's assumption that the additional benefit of a wealth increment diminishes as wealth increases was considered as a special case of the assumption of diminishing marginal utility; and Bernoulli's theory of decision-making under risk was seen as a natural way to extend marginal utility analysis from situations of certainty to situations of risk.

However, a number of problems remained open. The first involved the theory's capacity to account for the phenomenon of gambling. As Marshall (1890) noted, if Bernoulli's theory is correct and the marginal utility of money is diminishing, as he assumed it was, individuals ought not to gamble or play lotteries, even if these were actuarially fair, that is, even if their price were equal to their expected payoff. As we saw in Section 2.6.1, this was also one of the normative implications that Bernoulli drew from his own theory. However, Marshall observed, people do gamble and do buy lottery tickets, and thus the theory seems descriptively invalid. To solve the problem, he suggested that gambling could be explained by taking into account the pleasure or utility derived from the very activity of gambling. Yet this solution was at odds with utility theory itself: If the utility derived from the activity of gambling is relevant, should it not be explicitly included in a utility-based theory of decision under risk?

A second albeit much less severe problem concerned Bernoulli's logarithmic specification of the utility function for money. The Italian economist Vilfredo Pareto (1896), for instance, subscribed to Bernoulli's theory but argued that there is no reason to assume that the money utility function has a logarithmic form rather than, say, a square root form or some other concave functional form.

In the early decades of the twentieth century, skepticism about Bernoulli's theory increased. Frank Knight (1921) and John Maynard Keynes (1921) doubted that numerical probabilities completely capture the way in which individuals evaluate uncertain options and therefore had reservations about the possibility that the EU formula, which is based on numerical probabilities, can completely explain decisions under uncertainty. John Hicks (1931) and others argued that individuals evaluate risky alternatives by looking at the mean, the variance, and possibly other elements of the distribution of the uncertain payoffs rather than the expected utility of the payoffs. A further problem for EU came from the so-called ordinal turn in utility theory that took place in the period 1900–40.

Since the ordinal turn is relevant not only to understand the fortunes of Bernoulli's EU but also, in Sections 4 and 5, to comprehend the explanatory structure and the fortunes of von Neumann–Morgenstern's EU, I will discuss it in some detail.

3.3 The Ordinal Turn

The ordinal turn consisted of the gradual construction of a theory of demand, market equilibrium, and price that is independent of the assumption that utility is measurable, and thus of a theory shielded from the criticisms of the unmeasurability of utility mentioned in Section 3.1. The ordinal turn was initiated around 1900 by Pareto ([1906/9] 2014) and was significantly advanced in the early 1930s by Hicks and other economists, and by the late 1930s the ordinal approach became fully dominant in utility analysis.

There are two aspects in the ordinal turn that are often confused but that should be kept distinct: the move to a preference-based approach and the focus on an ordinal-utility function.

3.3.1 Preferences Are Primary

Regarding the first aspect, in the course of the ordinal turn the primary notion of economic analysis ceased to be the notion of marginal utility or that of utility and became the notion of "preference." Pareto and the other ordinalists assumed that individuals are always able to compare two options x and y and state which they prefer or, alternatively, to state that they are indifferent between them.

For the ordinalists, the notion of preferences has three advantages over the notion of utility. First, it overcomes discussions and criticisms of the proper definition of utility, that is, of whether utility should be identified with what satisfies needs, pleasures, or desires, selfish or unselfish as they might be. For the ordinalists, in fact, a preference ranking can express any type of taste: material or spiritual, selfish, altruistic, or even masochistic, healthy or unhealthy, moral or immoral.

Second, the notion of preference allows economists to remain agnostic about the psychology of the individual. Allegedly, when an individual faces different options he takes into account the need, the pleasure, the desirability, the healthiness, the morality, and other possible dimensions associated with each option; he evaluates and trades off these different dimensions through a complex psychological process and eventually arrives at defining his preferences among the options; finally, based on such preferences, the individual performs some economic act, that is, he purchases, sells, or exchanges some of the available options. The ordinalists claimed that only the eventual preferences are relevant for economic analysis, while the complex psychological processes that generated them might be relevant for the psychologist but not for the economist.

For the ordinalists, the third advantage of preference over utility is that, although the notion of preference remains a mental and thus not directly observable notion, it is connected to observable choice behavior more directly than the notion of utility. While the link between utility and choice is indirect, in the sense that it passes through the process of utility maximization, the link between preference and choice appears straightforward: If an individual prefers option x to option y, it is natural to assume that, other things being equal including the cost of the two options, when given the possibility the individual will choose x over y. Conversely, if the individual chooses x when y is also available, in general it seems plausible to infer from this act that he prefers x to y.

The consequence of all this is that in the preference-based approach, the notion of utility becomes ancillary: Utility only serves to represent the individual's preferences through numbers. That is, if (and only if) the individual prefers option x to option y, then the utility number $u(x)$ associated with x should be larger than the utility number $u(y)$ associated with y.

3.3.2 Rankings and Ordinal Utility

The second aspect of the ordinal turn is the one more directly associated with the label "ordinal." Ordinalists assume not only that individuals can rank the available options according to their preferences but also that individuals are unable to go beyond this type of ranking and make more sophisticated preference assessments. Thus, for example, ordinalists rule out that individuals can assess preference ratios and state, for instance, that they prefer option x three times as much as option y.

The assumption that individuals are only capable of ranking options allows for a significant degree of freedom in choosing the utility numbers $u(\cdot)$ that represent the individual's preferences: If (and only if) option x is preferred to option y, then the utility number $u(x)$ must be larger than the utility number $u(y)$, that is, $u(x) > u(y)$. But any numbers that satisfy this condition would do: It could be $u(x) = 10$ and $u(y) = 0$ or $u(x) = 1.000.000$ and $u(y) = -50,000$.

Pareto ([1906/9] 2014) provided a precise mathematical characterization of that degree of freedom: A utility function that represents the preference ranking between options, and only this ranking, is unique up to any (strictly) increasing transformation. This means that, if the utility function $u(x)$ only represents the individual's preference ranking, any other utility function $u^*(x) = F[u(x)]$, where F is any increasing function, also represents that preference ranking. For instance, if $u(x)$ represents the individual's preference ranking, then $u^*(x) = [u(x)]^2$ or $u^*(x) = \sqrt{u(x)}$ (assuming the range of $u(x)$ is positive) represent the same preference ranking. A function with this feature is called an "ordinal utility function."

3.3.3 Abandoning Diminishing Marginal Utility

Moving to an ordinal conception of utility is not without costs. In fact, all concepts and results that are not unique up to any increasing transformation, that is, all concepts and results that are substantially modified when the utility function is subjected to an increasing transformation, should be abandoned. The most important concept that should be abandoned is the one at the core of early utility theory: diminishing marginal utility.

To see why, consider the following example. An individual prefers three apples to two apples and prefers two apples to one apple. The utility index $u(x)$ representing this preference ranking should then satisfy the following property: $u(3 \ apples) > u(2 \ apples) > u(1 \ apple)$; for brevity, $u(3) > u(2) > u(1)$. For instance, it could be that $u(3) = 6$, $u(2) = 5$, and $u(1) = 3$. In this case, the marginal utility of the apples is diminishing: the marginal utility of the first apple is $3 - 0 = 3$, the marginal utility of the second apple is $5 - 3 = 2$, and the marginal utility of the third apple is $6 - 5 = 1$. But $u(x)$ is unique up to any increasing transformation, so that, for instance, $u^*(x) = [u(x)]^4$ also represents the individual's preferences regarding apples: $u^*(1) = 81$, $u^*(2) = 625$, and $u^*(3) = 1,296$, and in fact $u^*(3) > u^*(2) > u^*(1)$. However, the marginal utility of the apples is now increasing: the marginal utility of the first apple is $81 - 0 = 81$, the marginal utility of the second apple is $625 - 81 = 544$, and the marginal utility of the third apple is $1,296 - 625 = 671$.

3.3.4 Ordinal and Cardinal Utility

The two aspects of the ordinal turn – the move to a preference-based approach and the focus on an ordinal-utility function – are distinct in the sense that it is possible to maintain that preferences are the primary notion of economic analysis (and therefore that the utility function is only a convenient tool for representing preferences numerically) and, at the same time, to argue that individuals are capable of making preference assessments more sophisticated than the mere ranking of options. In this case, the degree of freedom with which utility numbers can be chosen diminishes and, correspondingly, the type of mathematical transformations to which the utility function can be submitted shrinks.

In particular, in the 1930s the discussion focused on the possibility that individuals can rank not only options but also "transitions" among options, that is, that individuals can state not only that they prefer option y to option x, and option z to option y, but also that they prefer moving from x to y more than they prefer moving from y to z. Economists focused on the capacity of ranking transitions because it would allow them to recover the notion of diminishing marginal utility. In fact, saying that an individual prefers moving from x to y more than he prefers moving from y to z is fundamentally equivalent to saying that, in that movement, the marginal utility of the options is diminishing.

The outcome of the discussion of the 1930s about the ranking of transitions among options was that, if individuals can rank transitions, and if some hypotheses about the relationship between preferences among options and preference among transitions are satisfied, then the utility function representing the individual's preferences is unique up to a subset of the increasing transformations, namely the *linearly* increasing transformations (for a reconstruction of that discussion, see Moscati 2013).[4]

This means that, if the utility function $u(x)$ represents the individual's preferences, any other utility function $u^*(x)$ obtained by multiplying $u(x)$ by a positive number α and then adding any number β, that is, a transformation $u^*(x) = \alpha u(x) + \beta$, with $\alpha > 0$, also represents the individual's preferences. For instance, if $u(x)$ represents the individual's preference ranking, $u^*(x) = 3u(x) + 5$ also represents that preference ranking. If the utility function is unique up to linearly increasing transformations, then it cannot be that the marginal utility is diminishing with a certain utility function $u(x)$ and increasing with a transformation $u^*(x)$ of it. That is, if the utility function is unique up to linearly increasing transformations, the notion of diminishing marginal utility can be rehabilitated.

In the late 1930s, a utility function that is unique up to linearly increasing transformations began to be called a "cardinal utility function," and this in contrast with ordinal utility functions that are unique up to any, even nonlinearly, increasing transformation. In the 1930s and 1940s, most ordinalists rejected the assumptions on preferences that induce cardinal utility. However, in the 1950s, cardinal utility gained acceptance, also thanks to the revival of EU in the von Neumann–Morgenstern version (see Section 5).

3.4 Bernoulli's Theory and the Ordinal Turn

After this long foray into the ordinal turn, we can return to EU and explain why the rise of the ordinal approach cast further shadow on Bernoulli's hypothesis. As Hicks (1934) and other economists pointed out, just like the notion of diminishing marginal utility, expected utility theory is also incompatible with an ordinal conception of utility, and this because if the utility function $u(x)$ representing the individual's preferences over the outcomes of the gambles is unique up to any increasing transformation, then the course of action associated with the highest expected utility might be undetermined.

To see the problem, consider the following example, which is similar to the example used in Section 3.3.3 to illustrate why diminishing marginal utility is not compatible with the ordinal approach. The preferences for money of a

---

[4] In the economic literature, the linearly increasing transformations are often called "positive affine transformations." In this Element, I prefer avoiding the technical term "affine" and stick to the more intuitive term "linearly increasing."

decision maker are represented by the utility function $u(x) = \sqrt{100 + x}$, where 100 is his initial wealth and x is the net amount of money that he can win or lose by participating in a gamble. Imagine that the gamble is an actuarially fair one, yielding a gain of 50 ducats or a loss of 50 ducats with an even chance. Apparently, according to EU the decision maker should not participate in the gamble because the expected utility associated with it, namely $\frac{1}{2}\sqrt{150} + \frac{1}{2}\sqrt{50}$, is smaller than the expected utility associated with not gambling, that is, $\sqrt{100}$. However, if the utility function $u(x)$ is ordinal in nature, the function $u^*(x) = [\sqrt{100 + x}]^4$, that is, $u^*(x) = [100 + x]^2$, also represents the decision maker's preferences. The problem is that now the expected utility of gambling, that is, $\frac{1}{2}[\sqrt{150}]^4 + \frac{1}{2}[\sqrt{50}]^4 = \frac{1}{2}150^2 + \frac{1}{2}50^2$, is larger than the expected utility of not gambling, that is, $[\sqrt{100}]^4 = 100^2$, and therefore the decision maker should now participate in the gamble.

Neither the decision maker's preferences for money nor his initial wealth has changed, and thus the contradictory indication of EU is problematic from both a normative viewpoint ("What should the decision maker do?") and a descriptive viewpoint ("What will the decision maker do?"). In other words, EU does not appear compatible with an ordinal conception of utility.

It is important to note that, as in the case of diminishing marginal utility, the problem would disappear if the utility function $u(x)$ were cardinal rather than ordinal in nature (see Section 3.3.4). That is, as is easily verified algebraically, if the expected utility of an option is higher than the expected utility of another option, a linearly increasing transformation of the utility function $u(x)$ would not modify such inequality. However, as already observed, the ordinalists of the 1930s and 1940s rejected cardinal utility.

The contrast between EU and the then dominant ordinal conception of utility, as well as the other criticisms discussed in Section 3.2, explains why in the late 1930s and early 1940s few economists supported EU. A clear manifestation of this state of affairs was that the two major economic treatises written in that period, Hicks's (1939) *Value and Capital* and Paul Samuelson's (1947) *Foundations of Economic Analysis* (completed around 1940), did not even mention EU.

The fortunes of EU began to recover in 1944, when von Neumann and Morgenstern put forward a novel, preference-based version of the theory.

4 Von Neumann and Morgenstern's EU: Presentation

John von Neumann (1903–57) was a Hungarian-American polymath who embraced the so-called axiomatic program launched by the mathematician David Hilbert around 1900. According to this program, the fundamental concepts and assumptions of any scientific discipline should be defined through a set of axioms, and the discipline's scientific statements should be obtained as logical implications of the axioms, that is, as theorems. In the 1920s and 1930s, von Neumann had applied the axiomatic approach to fields as diverse as mathematics, logic, geometry, and physics. Oskar Morgenstern (1902–77) was an Austrian-American economist who, in the 1920s and 1930s, had discussed the paradoxes associated with situations in which the actions of two economic agents depend on the prediction of each regarding the other's action. Von Neumann and Morgenstern met in Princeton in 1938 and engaged in several discussions about economic theory that eventually led them to coauthor a book titled *Theory of Games and Economic Behavior* (von Neumann & Morgenstern [1944] 1953; on the genesis of the book, see Leonard 1995).

Theory of Games made several seminal contributions to economic theory. First, it gave birth to the economic analysis of strategic behavior, that is, to game theory. Second, it introduced into economics the axiomatic approach, as well as convex analysis and other mathematical tools that added to the economist's traditional toolbox based on the differential calculus. Third, and this is the most important contribution of the book for our topic, von Neumann and Morgenstern put forward a preference-based, axiomatic version of EU. Essentially, they showed that if and only if the preferences of the decision maker between risky options satisfy certain axioms, then she will prefer the risky option associated with the highest mathematical expectation of a cardinal utility function $\tilde{u}(x)$. Note the tilde on the top of $\tilde{u}(x)$, which distinguishes it from the utility function $u(x)$ used by Bernoulli and the early utility theorists.

From around the mid-1940s to the mid-1950s, von Neumann and Morgenstern's version of EU was the subject of an intense debate in which all major utility theorists of the period took part (see Moscati 2016, 2018, chaps. 10–12). Among the questions addressed in the debate were: What is the exact content of the EU axioms? Are these axioms descriptively and/or normatively valid? If yes, should EU be rehabilitated as an adequate theory of decision-making under risk? How should the utility function $\tilde{u}(x)$ featured in von Neumann and Morgenstern's EU be interpreted? In particular, is the function $\tilde{u}(x)$ equivalent to the utility function $u(x)$ used by Bernoulli and the early utility theorists? If so, can economic theory abandon the ordinal utility approach, build utility analysis on the notion of cardinal utility, and thus recover non-ordinal notions such as diminishing marginal utility? In this section, I present von Neumann and Morgenstern's EU, while in Section 5 I'll address the above questions.

4.1 Lotteries

Like Bernoulli's, von Neumann and Morgenstern's theory concerns decision-making among risky options for which the probability $p(E_i)$ of each possible event is supposed to be objectively given and known by the decision maker. Following a standard terminology in decision theory, we will call risky options of this type "prospects" or "lotteries."

If, for brevity, the objective probability $p(E_i)$ of event E_i is indicated as p_i, then a lottery yielding outcome x_1 with probability p_1, outcome x_2 with probability p_2, and so on, can be represented as $[x_1, p_1;\ x_2, p_2; \ldots;\ x_N, p_N]$ and, given a utility function $\widetilde{u}(x)$, its expected utility can be written as $\sum_{i=1}^{N} \widetilde{u}(x_i) p_i$.

The possible outcomes x_i of a lottery can be commodities of any type, but we will focus on lotteries in which outcomes are amounts of money.

As in Bernoulli's EU, and in contrast to prospect theory (see Section 7), in von Neumann and Morgenstern's EU the decision maker is supposed to be interested in her final levels of wealth, that is, her initial wealth plus the monetary gain, or minus the monetary loss, associated with the lottery's outcome. However, for the sake of simplicity and following the standard way of presenting von Neumann and Morgenstern's EU, we will assume that the decision maker's initial wealth is equal to zero. Accordingly, the net monetary gain or loss x_i that the decision maker obtains if event E_i occurs coincides with her final wealth. It can be shown, nonetheless, that this simplification is without loss of generality: An initial wealth a different from zero can be easily reintroduced into the picture by replacing x_i with $a + x_i$ in the argument of the function $\widetilde{u}(x)$ without modifying the results and implications of the theory.

4.2 Preference As a Binary Relation

In contrast to Bernoulli's utility-based approach, and in accord with the preference-based approach that had risen to prominence during the ordinal turn of the 1930s (see Section 3), the primitive element of von Neumann and Morgenstern's theory is the notion of preference: They assume that individuals are able to compare any two lotteries L_1 and L_2 and state which they prefer or, alternatively, to state that they are indifferent between them. Preferences over lotteries and other risky options are usually called risk preferences and are contrasted with riskless preferences over commodity bundles or amounts of money available with certainty.

While Pareto and the ordinalists were happy with the commonsensical, and somehow vague, notion of preference, von Neumann and Morgenstern treated "preference" as an economic-theoretic notion whose nature and properties should be defined exactly through a set of axioms. In particular, they defined "preference" as a binary relation, that is, as a relation between any two entities, including lotteries. This binary relation can be indicated by the symbol $\succcurlyeq$, where the expression $L_1 \succcurlyeq L_2$ indicates that either the decision maker prefers lottery L_1 to lottery L_2 or that she is indifferent between the two. The symbol $\succ$ rules out the possibility of indifference: $L_1 \succ L_2$ means that the decision maker strictly prefers lottery L_1 to lottery L_2 and is not indifferent between the two.

4.3 Axioms

Another difference between von Neumann and Morgenstern's approach and the ordinalists' is that the latter took for granted that preferences can always be represented numerically by a utility function. Von Neumann and Morgenstern, in contrast, identified which properties, that is, which axioms, the binary relation $\succcurlyeq$ over the set of lotteries should satisfy not only to guarantee a numerical representation but also to warrant that such representation has the expected-utility form.

The discussion that followed the publication of *Theory of Games* clarified the meaning of the axioms originally put forward by von Neumann and Morgenstern and made explicit an assumption that remained implicit in their axiomatic system, an assumption that came to be called the "Independence Axiom" (for a reconstruction of that discussion, see Moscati 2016). Here, I will present the axiomatization of EU that stabilized in the early 1950s. In this axiomatization, there are five axioms – completeness, transitivity, continuity, reduction, and independence – and, as we will see in a moment, each of these axioms has a purely ordinal nature in the sense that it concerns only the ranking of options.

4.3.1 Completeness and Transitivity

The two basic properties that the preference relation $\succcurlyeq$ over lotteries should display are expressed by the axioms of completeness and transitivity.

Completeness requires that the decision maker can rank all lotteries in her choice set from the most preferred to the least preferred one. More formally, when faced with any two lotteries L_1 and L_2, the decision maker either prefers L_1 to L_2, or L_2 to L_1 or is indifferent between the two. In symbols, either $L_1 \succcurlyeq L_2$, or $L_2 \succcurlyeq L_1$, or both, and this for any two lotteries in the choice set. In the first place and almost tacitly, completeness assumes that the decision maker is already aware of all alternatives available to her, that is, that she does not need to engage in a preliminary search phase to identify the available alternatives. Secondly, completeness rules out that the decision maker is undecided between options.

Transitivity states that, if the decision maker prefers lottery L_1 to lottery L_2, and prefers lottery L_2 to lottery L_3, then she should also prefer lottery L_1 to lottery L_3. In symbols, if $L_1 \succcurlyeq L_2$ and $L_2 \succcurlyeq L_3$, then $L_1 \succcurlyeq L_3$. Transitivity rules out cyclical patterns of strict preferences, that is, situations in which $L_1 \succ L_2$, $L_2 \succ L_3$, and $L_3 \succ L_1$, which would make it tricky for the decision maker to say which lottery she prefers and thus choose. Taken together, and this is the important point, completeness and transitivity ensure that the decision maker can identify her most preferred lottery.

From a mathematical viewpoint, completeness and transitivity are necessary conditions to represent the decision maker's preference ranking through numbers. In fact, if completeness fails, that is, if the decision maker does not know what she prefers between, say, L_1 and L_2, it is not clear whether the number n_1 associated with lottery L_1 should be larger or smaller than the number n_2 associated with L_2. If transitivity fails, preference cycles such as $L_1 \succ L_2 \succ L_3 \succ L_1$ could occur. To reflect this ranking, the number n_1 associated with lottery L_1 should be larger than the number n_2 associated with L_2, n_2 should be larger than the number n_3 associated with L_3, and n_3 should be larger than n_1: $n_1 > n_2 > n_3 > n_1$. This, however, means that the number n_1 should be larger than itself, which is impossible.

4.3.2 Continuity

Completeness and transitivity are necessary but not sufficient conditions to represent the decision maker's preference ranking through a numerical function. Over rich enough sets, for sufficiency the continuity axiom is needed. This requires that small changes in the probability of the outcomes of the lotteries do not change (and this explains the "continuity" denomination) the decision maker's preference ranking between lotteries.

For instance, consider a decision maker who prefers gaining $100 to gaining $99. Now imagine introducing some risk into the picture: The $100 gain is not certain anymore but there exists a probability p, with $0 < p < 1$, that the decision maker will lose $10, which for her is worse than gaining $99. In other words, and using the notation introduced at the beginning of Section 4.1, the decision maker now faces a lottery $[-\$10, p; \$100, (1 - p)]$. The continuity axiom requires that, if the probability p of losing $10 is sufficiently small, the decision maker prefers the lottery $[-\$10, p; \$100, (1 - p)]$ to $99 for sure.

As already pointed out, if added to the axioms of completeness and transitivity, the continuity axiom ensures that the decision maker's preference ranking between lotteries can be represented by the ranking of utility numbers, and in this lies the main *raison d'être* of the axiom.

4.3.3 Reduction of Compound Lotteries

To illustrate the fourth assumption – the axiom of reduction of compound lotteries or, for brevity, the reduction axiom – we need to distinguish between simple and compound lotteries. In a simple lottery, the possible outcomes are commodities or amounts of money. In compound lotteries, some of the outcomes may be lotteries themselves.

An example of a compound lottery is a flip-the-coin game that yields $100 if the coin comes up heads; if the coin comes up tails, the player must flip the coin again: If heads obtains in the second round, she wins $100, while if tails obtains she gets nothing. This compound lottery can be written as $\left[\$100, \frac{1}{2}; L_2, \frac{1}{2}\right]$, where L_2 is the lottery $\left[\$100, \frac{1}{2}; \$0, \frac{1}{2}\right]$ played in the second round of the game.

A compound lottery can be reduced to a simple lottery that yields the same outcomes with the same overall probability. In the game of our example, the overall probability of winning $100 is equal to $\frac{1}{2} + \left(\frac{1}{2} \times \frac{1}{2}\right) = \frac{3}{4}$ and the overall probability of winning $0 is $\frac{1}{4}$. Therefore, the compound lottery $\left[\$100, \frac{1}{2}; L_2, \frac{1}{2}\right]$ can be reduced to the simple lottery $\left[\$100, \frac{3}{4}; \$0, \frac{1}{4}\right]$.

The reduction axiom requires that the decision maker is indifferent between a compound lottery and the simple lottery obtained from it by reduction. This axiom basically rules out the possibility that the decision maker's preferences between lotteries depend on factors such as pleasure or displeasure for longer gambling (compound lotteries last more than simple lotteries) or pleasure or displeasure for suspense (arguably, compound lotteries are more thrilling than simple lotteries).

More generally, the reduction axiom rules out that the decision maker's preferences between lotteries depend on the specific type of aleatory process characterizing the lotteries and requires the decision maker to care only about the final outcomes and overall probabilities characterizing each lottery. Thus, to consider a different example, the reduction axiom also requires the decision maker to be indifferent between possessing a single ticket in a lottery that has in total 20 tickets, and 10 tickets in a lottery that has in total 200 tickets, whereby both lotteries have the same unique prize. In both cases, in fact, the overall probability of getting the prize is $\frac{1}{20}$.

4.3.4 Independence Axiom

Samuelson (1950) christened the fifth EU postulate the "Independence Axiom." It is not required for representing the preference relation $\succeq$ over lotteries numerically, but it is the assumption that gives this representation its specific expected utility form $\sum \tilde{u}(x_i)p_i$. For this reason, it has been the most debated of the five EU axioms.

Intuitively, the Independence Axiom requires that the preference ranking between two lotteries does not depend on the parts that the lotteries have in common but only on the parts that distinguish them. More exactly, the Independence Axiom states that, for any three lotteries L_1, L_2, and L_3, if the decision maker prefers lottery L_1 to lottery L_2, then she should also prefer the compound lottery yielding L_1 with probability p and L_3 with probability $(1 - p)$, to the compound lottery yielding L_2 with probability p and L_3 with probability $(1 - p)$, and this for any probability p. More formally, the Independence Axiom states that, for any L_1, L_2, L_3, and for any $p \in (0, 1)$, $L_1 \succcurlyeq L_2$ if and only if $[L_1, p; \ L_3, (1 - p)] \succcurlyeq [L_2, p; \ L_3, (1 - p)]$.

To illustrate the axiom, consider three lotteries that yield, each with probability one, a trip to New York, a trip to London, and a trip to Venice, respectively. Imagine that the decision maker prefers the first lottery to the second, that is, she prefers a trip to New York to a trip to London. The Independence Axiom requires that the decision maker should also prefer the compound lottery yielding a trip to New York with probability p and a trip to Venice with probability $(1 - p)$, to the compound lottery yielding a trip to London with probability p and a trip to Venice with probability $(1 - p)$: if [New York,1] $\succcurlyeq$ [London,1], then [New York, p; Venice, $(1 - p)$] $\succcurlyeq$ [London, p; Venice, $(1 - p)$]. And this for any probability p and independently of how the decision maker ranks the trip to Venice with respect to the trip to New York and the trip to London.

The two compound lotteries differ for what happens with probability p (a trip to New York or a trip to London), while they have in common what happens with probability $(1 - p)$, that is, a trip to Venice. Thus, as already suggested, the Independence Axiom states that for the decision maker the parts common to both lotteries (here: Venice) cancel out and that her preference ranking only depends on what distinguishes the two lotteries (here: New York vs. London).

4.3.5 Independence Axiom versus Additivity Assumption

To further clarify the content of the Independence Axiom it is useful to contrast it with an apparently similar assumption that was made in early utility theories but abandoned by the early twentieth century: the assumption that the utilities of different commodities are additive or separable across goods (on the history of this assumption, see Moscati 2007). This means that the utility g of a riskless commodity bundle containing two goods, for example, a cup of coffee x and a croissant y, is given by the sum of the utility of the coffee and the utility of the croissant, as for instance in the following functional form: $g(x, y) = u(x) + u(y)$.

One main implication of the additivity assumption is that, if the decision maker prefers a glass of beer (call it z) to a cup coffee, that is, if for her $u(z) > u(x)$, then she must also prefer the commodity bundle beer-and-croissant (z, y) to the commodity bundle coffee-and-croissant (x, y), that is, for her $g(z, y) > g(x, y)$. In fact, under the additivity assumption $g(z, y) = u(z) + u(y)$ and $g(x, y) = u(x) + u(y)$; therefore, if $u(z) > u(x)$, then $u(z) + u(y) > u(x) + u(y)$.

The Independence Axiom and the additivity assumption are similar in the sense that both require that the preference ranking between two options, be they lotteries or commodity bundles, does not depend on the parts that the options have in common (trip to Venice; croissant) but only on the parts that distinguish them (New York or London; beer or coffee).

However, while the Independence Axiom seems plausible (at least at first sight), it is easy to see that the additivity assumption is not because it rules out the possible complementarity or substitutability between goods, that is, the circumstance that the utility of a good (e.g., a beer, a coffee) may depend on the concurrent availability of another good (e.g., a croissant). In our example, the decision maker may indeed prefer a glass of beer to a cup of coffee, but dislike drinking the beer while eating a croissant, and enjoy a coffee with a croissant. For this decision maker, $u(z) > u(x)$ but $g(z, y) < g(x, y)$.

Why does this problem not come up with the Independence Axiom? The reason is that, while the additivity assumption has to do with the *joint* consumption of different goods (coffee *and* croissant, beer *and* croissant), the Independent Axiom relates to the consumption of different goods in *mutually exclusive* situations (*either* a trip to New York *or* a trip to London). This mutual exclusion rules out the possibility that complementarity or substitutability relationships between goods enter the scene.

4.4 The EU Theorem

The core of the preference-based version of EU is a theorem, called the von Neumann–Morgenstern theorem, the EU theorem, or the EU representation theorem. The theorem states that, if the decision maker's binary preference relation $\succeq$ over lotteries satisfies the five axioms of (1) completeness, (2) transitivity, (3) continuity, (4) reduction of compound lotteries, and (5) independence, then (and only then) there exists a real-valued function $\tilde{u}(x)$ defined over the set of the outcomes of the lotteries, such that, for any two lotteries L_1 and L_2, the decision maker prefers L_1 to L_2 if and only if the mathematical expectation of the function $\tilde{u}(x)$ calculated with respect to L_1, that is,

$\sum_{L_1}\widetilde{u}(x_i)p_i$, is larger than the mathematical expectation of $\widetilde{u}(x)$ calculated with respect to L_2, that is, $\sum_{L_2}\widetilde{u}(x_i)p_i$. More succinctly, $L_1 \succcurlyeq L_2$ if and only if $\sum_{L_1}\widetilde{u}(x_i)p_i \geq \sum_{L_2}\widetilde{u}(x_i)p_i$.

The axioms also imply that the function $\widetilde{u}(x)$ satisfies the basic ordinalist condition required to be interpreted as a utility function, namely that the decision maker prefers outcome x to outcome y, that is, $x \succcurlyeq y$, if and only if $\widetilde{u}(x) \geq \widetilde{u}(y)$. Since $\widetilde{u}(x)$ is a utility function, the mathematical expectations $\sum_{L_1}\widetilde{u}(x_i)p_i$ and $\sum_{L_2}\widetilde{u}(x_i)p_i$ can be interpreted as the expected utilities associated, respectively, with lottery L_1 and lottery L_2. Moreover, the axioms imply that the utility function $\widetilde{u}(x)$ is cardinal in nature, that is, unique up to linearly increasing transformations of the form $a\widetilde{u}(x) + \beta$, with $a > 0$.

To distinguish the function $\widetilde{u}(x)$ featured in von Neumann and Morgenstern's EU from the utility function $u(x)$ featured in Bernoulli's EU, the former is usually called the von Neumann–Morgenstern utility function. In Section 5.6, we will discuss the relationships between $\widetilde{u}(x)$ and $u(x)$.[5]

4.5 Two Comments

Before moving on to the discussion of von Neumann and Morgenstern's EU, two final comments are in order. First, the specificity of von Neumann and Morgenstern's version of EU is not so much that it is axiomatic but that the axioms are on preferences rather than the utility function. In fact, it is possible to construct an axiomatic version of Bernoulli's EU, where the axioms directly concern, and posit restrictions upon, a Bernoullian utility function $u(x)$ defined over the set of the lottery's outcomes. In this approach, sometimes called the "direct approach" to the axiomatization of EU (see Peterson 2017), if the decision maker's utility function $u(x)$ satisfies certain axioms, then she will prefer the lottery associated with the highest expected utility value $\sum u(x_i)p_i$.

The direct approach to axiomatic EU, however, never took hold in economics. One reason is that it is in contrast with the preference-based approach that has dominated the economic analysis of individual decision-making since the ordinal turn of the 1930s (see Section 3). Moreover, the descriptive and normative validity of some of the axioms in the direct approach is problematic, arguably even more problematic than the axioms used in von Neumann and Morgenstern's preference-based approach (for a discussion, see Peterson 2004).

---

[5] Unfortunately, the terminology is not standardized. For example, in their popular microeconomic textbook Mas-Colell, Whinston, and Green (2005, chap. 6) call the function $\sum \widetilde{u}(x)p_i$ defined over the set of lotteries the "von Neumann–Morgenstern expected utility function," and the function $\widetilde{u}(x)$ defined over the set of the lotteries' outcomes the "Bernoulli utility function." As discussed at length in Section 5.6, I argue that calling $\widetilde{u}(x)$ the Bernoulli utility function is misleading.

The second, more technical comment is that the cardinal character of the function $\widetilde{u}(x)$ does not draw from the EU axioms, which are in fact ordinal in nature, but from the fact that we want to represent the decision maker's preference ranking over lotteries in terms of a specific mean of $\widetilde{u}(x)$, namely the arithmetic mean. If we allow for the possibility of different means, such as the geometric or the harmonic mean, the cardinal restriction disappears.

Thus, if we take an increasing, nonlinear transformation of $\widetilde{u}(x)$ such as $v(x) = 10^{\widetilde{u}(x)}$ and couple it with the geometric mean of $v(x)$, we not only have that $L_1 \succcurlyeq L_2$ if and only if $\sum_{L_1} \widetilde{u}(x_i)p_i \geq \sum_{L_2} \widetilde{u}(x_i)p_i$ but also if and only if $\prod_{L_1} [v(x_i)]^{p_i} \geq \prod_{L_2} [v(x_i)]^{p_i}$, that is, if and only if the geometric mean of $v(x)$ calculated with respect to L_1 is larger than the geometric mean of $v(x)$ calculated with respect to L_2 (for a discussion, see Montesano 1985).

However, probably because it is difficult to attach a psychological meaning to numerical representations of preference rankings in terms of geometric or harmonic means, these alternative representations have not played any significant role in the history of decision theory.

5 Von Neumann and Morgenstern's EU: Discussion

Since its appearance in the mid-1940s, von Neumann and Morgenstern's EU has been the subject of an intense debate. The first and most intense phase of the debate lasted until the mid-1950s, but discussions on the theory, its exact scope and meaning, its relationship with Bernoulli's EU, its descriptive and normative validity, and the theoretical status of its components have continued until the present. In this section, I offer an interpretative review of this rich discussion with a focus on its methodological dimension.

5.1 Explanatory Structure and Decision Mechanism

5.1.1 Unexplained Risk Preferences

We already pointed out that von Neumann and Morgenstern's theory does not explain why decision makers prefer one lottery to another. Thus, the theory does not state that a decision maker prefers a certain lottery to another because, say, for him the marginal utility of money is diminishing, or because he does not like taking a risk, or because he is afraid of losing money. Rather, in von Neumann and Morgenstern's theory the decision maker's preferences between lotteries, also called risk preferences, are the primitive and unexplained element of the analysis.

5.1.2 A Preference-Based Mechanism

The decision mechanism posited by von Neumann and Morgenstern's EU is also different from the multiply-and-add mechanism posited by Bernoulli's EU. As discussed in Section 2.7.5, in the latter the decision maker is supposed to multiply the utility of each outcome by its probability, to add the values $u(x_i)p_i$ in order to calculate the expected utility $\sum u(x_i)p_i$ of the lottery, and finally to compare the expected utilities of different lotteries in order to choose the one with the highest $\sum u(x_i)p_i$.

In the von Neumann-Morgenstern, preference-based version of EU, the decision mechanism is different and, at least apparently, simpler: Based on his complete and transitive preferences, the decision maker ranks all lotteries in his choice set from the most preferred to the least preferred and chooses the most preferred one. No calculation is required.

5.2 Risk Attitudes

A further way to appreciate the differences between von Neumann and Morgenstern's EU and Bernoulli's is to see how the decision makers' attitudes toward risk are conceptualized in the two versions of EU.

In the debate on EU following the publication of *Theory of Games*, Milton Friedman and Leonard Jimmie Savage (1948) made explicit notions of risk aversion and risk-seeking that were already present, although tacitly, in Bernoulli's analysis. For Friedman and Savage, a decision maker is risk-averse if he prefers a sure amount of money \$K to a lottery whose expected payoff is \$K and is risk-seeking if that preference goes in the opposite direction.

This definition of risk attitudes, sometimes called *actuarial definition of risk attitudes*, rapidly became central to decision theory. Two quick comments on it are in order. First, it is a definition in line with the spirit of the ordinal turn: It is based on preferences rather than utility, and it relies exclusively on preference rankings of lotteries without bringing into play more sophisticated preference assessments, such as the preference ranking of transitions between lotteries (see Section 3.3.4). Second, the definition is "model-free," that is, independent of the validity of EU, and therefore it can be used also if one adopts an alternative theory of decision-making under risk such as, say, prospect theory (see Section 7).

In von Neumann and Morgenstern's EU, the fact that a decision maker prefers having \$K for sure rather than participating in a lottery with an expected payoff of \$K (so being actuarially risk-averse) or that another decision maker prefers participating in the lottery (so being actuarially risk-seeking) is a direct expression of the decision maker's risk preferences. Therefore, just like risk preferences, risk attitudes are also a primitive element of the analysis. This means that risk attitudes can be employed to explain a number of economic phenomena, such as the demand and supply for insurance, but remain themselves unexplained. Since in von Neumann and Morgenstern's EU there is a tight correspondence between risk preferences and risk attitudes, decision theorists tend to talk of them interchangeably.

Speaking of correspondences, in Section 2.7.3 we observed that in Bernoulli's EU there is a one-to-one correspondence between the curvature of the utility function $u(x)$ and the decision maker's attitude toward risk: The decision maker is actuarially risk-averse (risk-seeking) if and only if $u(x)$ is concave (convex). A similar correspondence exists in von Neumann and Morgenstern's EU: The decision maker is actuarially risk-averse (risk-seeking) if and only if $\tilde{u}(x)$ is concave (convex). However, in von Neumann and Morgenstern's EU this correspondence *does not* indicate a causal relationship of the type: "*Since* the utility function $u(x)$ is concave, *then* the individual is risk averse." Here, the relationship goes in the opposite direction: "Since the decision maker has risk-averse preferences, then the utility function $\tilde{u}(x)$ that is used to represent them is concave." Moreover, as will be discussed in Section 5.6, the curvature of the function $\tilde{u}(x)$ cannot be interpreted as indicating diminishing or increasing marginal utility of money.

5.3 The Descriptive and Normative Validity of the Axioms

In the last seventy-five years, the descriptive and normative validity of each of the five axioms of von Neumann and Morgenstern's EU has been disputed. In the late 1940s and early 1950s, however, the discussion focused on the Independence Axiom. Following the history of EU, I first examine the discussion on the validity of this axiom and then move on to the debate on the other axioms.

5.3.1 Independence Axiom

In the early debate on the EU axioms, the validity of the axioms of completeness, transitivity, continuity, and reduction was more or less taken for granted. Accordingly, the validity of von Neumann and Morgenstern's EU was seen as depending on the validity of the remaining axiom, the Independence Axiom.

Samuelson (1950) initially rejected EU because he considered the Independence Axiom a descriptively implausible and normatively unjustified assumption. However, in discussions with other economists such as Marschak, Friedman, and Savage, Samuelson became persuaded of the normative validity of the Axiom, and this brought him to accept EU, at least as a normative theory of rational decision-making under risk (see Moscati 2016). The reason why Samuelson eventually accepted the Independence Axiom, and thus EU, is that Savage convinced him that the Axiom is a special case of a normatively compelling principle, which Savage later called the Sure-Thing principle (see Section 6).

Savage considered three outcomes, x_1, x_2, and x_3, two mutually exclusive events, E_i and E_j, and two courses of action, A_1 and A_2. A_1 yields outcome x_1 in the event E_i and outcome x_3 in the event E_j: $A_1 = [x_1, E_i; \, x_3, E_j]$. Course of action A_2 yields outcome x_2 in the event E_i and, just like A_1, outcome x_3 in the event E_j: $A_1 = [x_2, E_i; \, x_3, E_j]$. Savage argued that if the decision maker prefers outcome x_1 to outcome x_2, it would be rational for him to prefer course of action A_1 to A_2, because by doing so he guarantees that whichever event occurs he won't be worse off.

In the early 1950s, Marschak (1950), Samuelson (1952), Savage (Friedman and Savage 1952) and the majority of other economists accepted the Independence Axiom as normatively compelling and, accordingly, advocated EU as a sound normative theory for rational behavior under risk. Concerning the descriptive validity of the Independence Axiom, Samuelson and most other economists remained agnostic.

5.3.2 The Allais Paradox

In the early 1950s, the main opponent of EU and the Independence Axiom was the French economist Maurice Allais. Allais (1953) presented a choice situation that later became known as the "Allais paradox," in which the majority of people not only violate EU but also appear to have good reasons for doing that. Moreover, if one accepts all other axioms of EU, the violation of EU appears due to a violation of the Independence Axiom.

Allais imagined two pairs of lotteries whose monetary payoffs were expressed in French francs, a currency substituted by the euro in 2002. To make the choice situation conceived by Allais more comprehensible to readers, here I express monetary payoffs in euros rather than francs. The first pair of lotteries consists of lottery L_1, which pays 100 million euros with probability one, and lottery L_2, which yields 500 million euros with probability $\frac{10}{100}$, 100 million euros with probability $\frac{89}{100}$, and zero euros with probability $\frac{1}{100}$. The second pair consists of lottery L_3, which yields 100 million euros with probability $\frac{11}{100}$ and zero euros with probability $\frac{89}{100}$, and lottery L_4, which yields 500 million euros with probability $\frac{10}{100}$ and zero euros with probability $\frac{90}{100}$.

Allais contended that the majority of individuals prefer L_1 to L_2 and L_4 to L_3. They prefer L_1 to L_2 because they prefer to have 100 million euros with certainty rather than incurring in the possibility, however remote, of getting nothing. And they prefer L_4 to L_3 because both lotteries involve risk and the possibility of getting nothing. But while the probability of winning or getting nothing is very similar for the two lotteries, the prize that can be obtained by choosing L_4 (500 million euros) is five times as large as the prize that can be obtained by choosing L_3 (100 million euros). Thus, preferring L_1 to L_2 and L_4 to L_3 appears to be not only a common preference pattern but also one that cannot be easily labeled as "irrational." This preference pattern, however, violates EU.

One way to see this is to notice that, according to EU, preferring L_1 to L_2 implies that $\widetilde{u}(100{,}000{,}000) > \frac{10}{100}\widetilde{u}(500{,}000{,}000) + \frac{89}{100}\widetilde{u}(100{,}000{,}000) + \frac{1}{100}\widetilde{u}(0)$, and preferring L_4 to L_3 implies that $\frac{10}{100}\widetilde{u}(500{,}000{,}000) + \frac{90}{100}\widetilde{u}(0) > \frac{11}{100}\widetilde{u}(100{,}000{,}000) + \frac{89}{100}\widetilde{u}(0)$. However, there exists no utility function $\widetilde{u}(x)$ satisfying both inequalities, which implies that this pair of preferences violates EU.

A second, and for us more interesting, way to see that that preference pattern violates EU is to observe that, if one accepts all other axioms of EU, and in particular transitivity and reduction of compound lotteries, that pattern violates the Independence Axiom. The proof won't be given here, but the basic idea is that the Independence Axiom implies that, if the decision maker prefers L_1 to L_2, he should also prefer L_1 to a lottery that yields 500 million euros with probability $\frac{10}{11}$ and zero euros with probability $\frac{1}{11}$; in turn, if he prefers L_1 to this lottery, again by the Independence Axiom he should prefer L_3 to L_4. Therefore, if the decision maker prefers L_1 to L_2 and L_4 to L_3, his preferences cannot satisfy the Independence Axiom. From a normative viewpoint, as already noted, preferring L_1 to L_2 and L_4 to L_3, and thus violating the Independence Axiom, does not seem irrational.

At any rate, until at least the mid-1960s the Allais paradox had a negligible impact on decision theory and did not undermine the then dominant confidence in EU and the normative validity of the Independence Axiom.

5.3.3 Completeness

Moving on to the axiom of completeness and its descriptive validity, several scholars have pointed out that it can be violated because decision makers often are not aware of all prospects available to them (see, e.g., Gilboa, Postlewaite, & Schmeidler 2021). Moreover, even if they are aware of all available options, they may not know what they prefer and be indeed undecided (Gilboa, Postlewaite, & Schmeidler 2012).

Even from a normative viewpoint, as several scholars have argued, it is hard to claim that an individual with incomplete preferences is irrational. For instance, Aumann (1962, 446) wrote:

Does "rationality" demand that an individual make definite preference comparisons between all possible lotteries …? For example, certain decisions that our individual is asked to make might involve highly hypothetical situations, which he will never face in real life; he might feel that he cannot reach an "honest" decision in such cases. Other decision problems might be extremely complex, too complex for intuitive "insight," and our individual might prefer to make no decision at all in these problems.

5.3.4 Transitivity

Considering transitivity and its descriptive validity, this assumption may be violated when choice options contain multiple dimensions. For instance, when the two basic dimensions of lotteries (monetary payoffs and their probabilities) are inversely correlated (the higher the payoff, the lower the probability of obtaining it), intransitive preference patterns are rather frequent (Tversky 1969).

Unlike completeness, transitivity has been defended using normative arguments, the most important of which is the so-called money pump argument, originally advanced by Davidson, McKinsey, and Suppes (1955). Basically, the argument shows that an individual with intransitive preferences could be induced to pay money for nothing. Critics of the argument, however, have stressed that money pumping can become real only if a series of additional but implausible assumptions are made, so that the normative defense of transitivity based on that argument is weak (for an overview of the discussion, see Gustafsson 2022).

5.3.5 Continuity

At first sight, it seems easy to construct an example that calls into question the descriptive and normative validity of the continuity axiom. Reconsider the situation of Section 4.3.2, in which, however, the worst option is no longer "losing \$10" but "death." Arguably, for the decision maker $\$100 \succ \$99 \succ$ death, and one may claim that no probability p exists, however small it might be, such that the decision maker prefers lottery $[\text{death}, p; \$100, (1-p)]$ to \$99 for sure. If this were the case, the continuity axiom would be violated.

However, as noted by Luce and Raiffa (1957) and others, most of us, if we see a \$1 bill on the other side of the street, would gladly cross the street to pick up the bill. And this despite the fact that there is some probability p, although very small, that in the crossing we get hit by a car and die. Therefore, so the argument goes, much of our behavior shows that we are indeed willing to take a little risk to obtain something we like more, that is, in our example, that there indeed exists a sufficiently small probability p such that we prefer the lottery [death, p; $100, $(1 - p)$] to $99 for sure. This indicates that, contrary to first impressions, the continuity axiom is descriptively valid. And even from a normative viewpoint, it would be hard to consider a decision maker who crosses the street to pick up a $1 bill as irrational.

5.3.6 Reduction

Finally, concerning the axiom of reduction of compound lotteries, a series of experiments has shown that it is often violated (see, e.g., Kahneman & Tversky 1979; Abdellaoui, Klibanoff, & Placido 2015; Harrison, Martínez-Correa, & Swarthout 2015).

From a normative viewpoint, the reduction axiom could be defended by using a variation of the money pump argument discussed in Section 5.3.4. However, as in the case of violations of transitivity, a decision maker violating the reduction axiom could be induced to pay money for nothing only if a series of additional but implausible assumptions are made. Therefore, the normative defense of reduction based on the money pump argument is also weak (for a discussion, see Segal 1992).

5.4 Stability Issues

There are some further problems. The completeness and transitivity of preferences between risky options would be of little use in explaining or predicting the decision maker's choices if preferences are unstable over time, across choice domains, or across elicitation methods. Consider, for example, a decision maker whose preferences are complete and transitive at each moment but temporally unstable: on Monday, for him $L_1 \succ L_2 \succ L_3$, on Tuesday $L_2 \succ L_1 \succ L_3$, and on Wednesday $L_3 \succ L_2 \succ L_1$. What will he prefer and choose on Thursday?

5.4.1 Temporal Stability

Concerning the issue of temporal stability, a series of studies have shown that preferences between lotteries are, in fact, relatively stable (Andersen et al. 2008; Zeisberger, Vreko, & Langer 2012). In contrast, as I explain next, neither stability across domains nor stability across elicitation methods can be taken for granted.

5.4.2 Stability across Choice Domains

With respect to stability across choice domains, one aspect of the problem goes under the name of "menu effects" (Huber, Payne, & Puto 1982; Simonson 1989). Generally speaking, menu effects occur when adding or subtracting options from the menu, that is, from the choice set, appears to modify the decision maker's preferences. Sometimes it is possible to make sense of these modifications within the preference-based approach, but not always. In the case of preferences between lotteries, menu effects occur if the decision maker prefers lottery L_1 when faced with a choice set containing lottery L_1 and lottery L_2 only, but prefers lottery L_2 to lottery L_1 if lottery L_3 is added to the choice set. A number of studies suggest that preferences between lotteries are affected by menu effects (see, e.g., Herne 1999; Beauchamp et al. 2020).

Another form of preference instability across domains relates to the possibility that the decision maker's attitude toward risk changes when he is faced with options of different types. For instance, the decision maker might be more risk-averse when he chooses among insurance coverages for his home than when he chooses among insurance coverages for his car. As discussed in Section 5.2, in von Neumann and Morgenstern's EU the decision maker's risk attitudes are a direct expression of his preferences between lotteries, and therefore if risk attitudes are unstable over choice domains, risk preferences also are. A number of experimental studies document the instability of risk preference over choice domains (see Barseghyan, Prince, & Teitelbaum 2011; Einav et al. 2012).

5.4.3 Stability across Elicitation Methods

The third stability issue relates to the circumstance that the decision maker's preferences between lotteries appear to depend on the method that is used to elicit them. That is, when the elicitation method changes, preferences also seem to change. The most famous instance of preference instability across elicitation methods is related to the phenomenon of "preference reversal," first documented by Lichtenstein and Slovic (1971) and confirmed in several subsequent studies.

What happens is that, if the preferences of a group of individuals between lotteries of a certain type are elicited by asking them which lottery they prefer, the majority declare to prefer L_1 to L_2. If, however, the same decision makers are asked to state their willingness to pay to participate in each lottery, a significant part of those who preferred L_1 to L_2 say that they are willing to pay more to participate in L_2 than in L_1. From the viewpoint of economic theory, however, the two methods for eliciting preferences, namely the direct ranking of lotteries or their pricing, are equivalent and should therefore provide the same outcome. According to Lichtenstein and Slovic (2006), the phenomenon of preference reversal not only shows that preferences may be unstable across elicitation methods but, more fundamentally, calls into question the very existence of preferences as a stable psychological trait of decision makers.

5.4.4 Completeness, Transitivity, and Stability: Summing Up

To sum up the discussion in Sections 5.3 and 5.4, the descriptive validity of the axioms concerning the completeness and transitivity of preferences between lotteries, as well as the descriptive validity of the tacit assumption that these preferences are stable over time, across choice domains, and across elicitation methods, is dubious. As I will argue in Section 5.9, this state of affairs makes it questionable to interpret von Neumann and Morgenstern's risk preferences as psychologically realistic entities.

5.5 The Descriptive Validity of EU As a Whole

Independently of the validity of the EU assumptions, that is, even if the axioms or the implicit stability hypotheses of EU are not satisfied or even if individuals make decisions by applying some heuristic rule that does not involve preference or utility maximization, their choice behavior under risk can still be correctly described by using the EU formula $\sum \widetilde{u}(x_i)p_i$.[6] In this case, the theory considered as a whole would be descriptively valid.

To rationalize this descriptive validity, one may argue that individuals behave *as if* they calculated and compared the expected utility of lotteries, or, for von Neumann and Morgenstern's preference-based EU, that individuals behave *as if* they had stable risk preferences satisfying the five EU axioms. The as-if interpretation of EU was originally advanced by Friedman and Savage (1948) and refined and extended to other economic theories by Friedman (1953). We will discuss it in more detail in Sections 5.8 and 5.9. Here, we focus on the question of whether EU as a whole can be considered as descriptively valid.

5.5.1 Testing EU: Theory

There are different methods to test the descriptive validity of EU. One method is that used by Allais: The decision maker, call her Sarah, is faced with a series of binary choices between lotteries – L_1 vs. L_2, L_3 vs. L_4, and so on – and then it is checked whether there exists a utility function $\widetilde{u}(x)$ such that the lotteries chosen by Sarah are associated with higher values of the EU formula $\sum \widetilde{u}(x_i)p_i$. If such a utility function $\widetilde{u}(x)$ exists, EU is validated; otherwise, as it happens in the Allais paradox, EU is descriptively invalid.

---

[6] Simple heuristic rules for decision-making under risk that do not involve preference or utility maximization include the minimax rule (choose the lottery with the highest minimum payoff) and the maximax rule (choose the lottery with the highest maximum payoff). More sophisticated rules include the similarity heuristic (Rubinstein 1988) and the priority heuristic (Brandstätter, Gigerenzer, & Hertwig 2006).

A second, more indirect testing approach passes through the elicitation of the decision maker's utility function $\widetilde{u}(x)$. The general idea is to use the decision maker's choices over a first set of lotteries to estimate some values of $\widetilde{u}(x)$, to put the estimated values into the expression $\sum \widetilde{u}(x_i)p_i$, and to use this expression to predict the decision maker's choices over a second set of lotteries. If the predictions are correct, EU is validated; otherwise, it is violated.

There are different ways of eliciting the utility function $\widetilde{u}(x)$ from the decision maker's choices. Here, we consider the so-called certainty equivalence method, which works as follows. Our decision-maker Sarah is faced with a monetary lottery, say, [$0,0.5; $1,000,0.5], and asked to identify the certainty equivalent of the lottery, that is, the amount of money $K that makes her indifferent between playing the lottery and receiving $K for certain. Imagine that for Sarah the certainty equivalent of the lottery is $330, that is, she is indifferent between playing lottery [$0,0.5; $1,000,0.5] and $330. If EU is valid, then it must be that for her $\widetilde{u}(\$330) = 0.5 \times \widetilde{u}(\$0) + 0.5 \times \widetilde{u}(\$1,000)$. Notice that since $330 is less than the lottery's expected payoff, which is $500, Sarah is actuarially risk-averse.

As discussed in Section 4.4, the utility function $\widetilde{u}(x)$ is unique up to linearly increasing transformations of the form $a\widetilde{u}(x) + \beta$, with $\alpha > 0$. The two parameters α and β are arbitrary, and this makes it possible to fix two values of $\widetilde{u}(x)$ in a convenient way without loss of generality. For instance, we can state that $\widetilde{u}(\$0) = 0$ and $\widetilde{u}(\$1,000) = 10$. By inserting these two values into the EU formula, we find that $\widetilde{u}(\$330) = 0.5 \times 0 + 0.5 \times 10 = 5$.

We can repeat the exercise considering a different lottery, say, [$0, 0.2; $1,000, 0.8], and asking Sarah to identify its certainty equivalent; imagine Sarah says that it is $660. Then, by applying the EU formula, we can state that for her $\widetilde{u}(\$660) = 0.2 \times 0 + 0.8 \times 10 = 8$. Figure 1 represents the values of Sarah's utility function $\widetilde{u}(x)$ elicited so far.

Consider now the two lotteries [$330,0.5; $660,0.5] and [$0,0.4; $1,000,0.6]. Based on the values of $\widetilde{u}(x)$ calculated in the previous two steps, their expected utilities are, respectively, $0.5 \times 5 + 0.5 \times 8 = 6.5$ and $0.4 \times 0 + 0.6 \times 10 = 6$. Since the expected utility of [$330,0.5; $660,0.5] is larger than the expected utility of [$0,0.4; $1,000,0.6], EU predicts that Sarah will choose the former. If this is the case, EU is validated; otherwise, it is violated.

5.5.2 Testing EU: History

Experiments aimed at testing the descriptive validity of EU as a whole began in the early 1950s, with a pioneering experiment conducted by Mosteller and Nogee (1951). Without entering here into the rich story of the experimental tests of EU

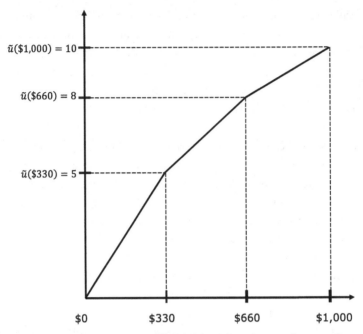

Figure 1 Sarah's utility function $\widetilde{u}(x)$ elicited from her preferences between lotteries.

conducted in the last seventy years or so (more on this in Schoemaker 1982; Starmer 2000; Moscati 2018), we can say that the findings of the experiments conducted until the mid-1960s were interpreted by the majority of decision theorists as supporting the descriptive validity of EU. The already discussed experiment by Allais (1953) and a thought experiment by Ellsberg (1961) called attention to patterns of choice violating EU (on Ellsberg's experiment, see Section 6). However, until the mid-1960s the experiments by Allais and Ellsberg were dismissed as dealing with very idiosyncratic situations.

Starting in the mid-1960s, a novel series of experiments showed that the choice patterns indicated by Allais and Ellsberg were frequent and systematic and called attention to further choice patterns violating EU. This experimental evidence undermined the earlier confidence in the descriptive validity of EU and prompted the search for alternative models of choice under risk and uncertainty that began in the mid-1970s and that is still going on (see Section 7).

5.6 The Interpretation of $\widetilde{u}(x)$

In the previous section, we discussed a way to elicit some values of the function $\widetilde{u}(x)$, such as $\widetilde{u}(\$0) = 0$, $\widetilde{u}(\$330) = 5$, $\widetilde{u}(\$660) = 8$, and $\widetilde{u}(\$1,000) = 10$. But how can these values be interpreted? In particular, can they be interpreted as indicating the utility that the decision maker attaches to the monetary amounts $0, $330, $660, and $1,000 possessed without uncertainty, that is, for certain?

Notice that Sarah's utility function $\widetilde{u}(x)$ is concave. Accordingly, if it is possible to interpret the values of $\widetilde{u}(x)$ as expressing the utility of riskless money, for Sarah the marginal utility of money would be diminishing. In effect, for her the marginal utility of the first $330 is equal to $\widetilde{u}(\$330) - \widetilde{u}(\$0) = 5 - 0 = 5$, the marginal utility of the additional $330 is $\widetilde{u}(\$660) - \widetilde{u}(\$330) = 8 - 5 = 3$, and the marginal utility of the additional $340 is $\widetilde{u}(\$1,000) - \widetilde{u}(\$660) = 10 - 8 = 2$. Is this interpretation warranted by von Neumann and Morgenstern's EU?

5.6.1 Two Distinct Functions

In the early 1950s, the discussion about the proper interpretation of the function $\widetilde{u}(x)$ represented an important part of the more general debate on von Neumann and Morgenstern's EU. The outcome of the discussion (see Moscati 2016, 2018) was that, in general, the function $\widetilde{u}(x)$ featuring in von Neumann and Morgenstern's EU is *not* equivalent to the utility function $u(x)$ for riskless money featured in Bernoulli's EU. It is true that both functions order options in the same way, in the sense that if the individual prefers outcome x_1 to outcome x_2, then $u(x_1) > u(x_2)$ and $\widetilde{u}(x_1) > \widetilde{u}(x_2)$. However, the similarity stops there.[7]

In particular, the curvatures of the two functions *need not be equal*: $\widetilde{u}(x)$ can be concave while $u(x)$ can be convex or linear, and vice versa. Therefore, the fact that Sarah's function $\widetilde{u}(x)$ is concave cannot be interpreted as indicating that for her the marginal utility of money is diminishing. It could well be the case that for Sarah the marginal utility of money is constant or even increasing, so that $u(x)$ is linear or even convex, while $\widetilde{u}(x)$ is concave.

5.6.2 Why $\widetilde{u}(x)$ and $u(x)$ Are Distinct

The fundamental reason why $\widetilde{u}(x)$ and $u(x)$ are not equivalent (apart from the way in which they rank options) is that $\widetilde{u}(x)$ is elicited from the decision maker's preferences between lotteries and therefore reflects and conflates all possible factors that may influence her preferences between uncertain options. For sure, one of these factors is Sarah's desire for money, which is the factor captured by the riskless utility function $u(x)$. But $\widetilde{u}(x)$ may also reflect other

---

[7] As illustrated by Okasha (2016), in the philosophical literature dealing with EU, $\widetilde{u}(x)$ and $u(x)$ are often confused, and von Neumann and Morgenstern's $\widetilde{u}(x)$ is typically identified with Bernoulli's $u(x)$. Okasha discusses some possible reasons for this confusion and points out the shortcomings it creates in the interpretation and normative use of EU.

factors, such as Sarah's specific attitude toward risk, the pleasure or displeasure she may associate with the very act of gambling, the worry for the regret she might feel if she chooses the lottery and eventually gets $0, and possibly other factors.

In our example, the fact that $\widetilde{u}(x)$ is concave tells us that Sarah prefers a sure amount of money $K to a lottery whose expected payoff is $K. Thus, she prefers $500 for sure to the lottery [$0,0.5; $1,000, 0.5]. The point is that this preference, and the associated concavity of $\widetilde{u}(x)$, may reflect a dislike that Sarah has for risky situations, maybe because she is an anxious person, rather than a diminishing marginal utility of money, which for her could be constant or even increasing. Alternatively, one can imagine that although Sarah is not an anxious person and for her the marginal utility of money is constant or even increasing, she prefers $500 for sure to playing the lottery [$0,0.5; $1,000,0.5] because for moral or religious reasons Sarah dislikes the very act of gambling. Still alternatively, one can imagine that Sarah is not an anxious person, that for her the marginal utility of money is constant or even increasing, that her moral or religious scruples do not preclude gambling, but that she prefers $500 for sure because she is afraid of the regret she may experience if she chooses the lottery and, in the end, gets $0.

The basic problem this example points out is that, within EU, it is not possible to disentangle the diverse factors that may influence the decision maker's preferences between lotteries. From a mathematical viewpoint, this problem manifests itself in the fact that the EU model has only one "free variable," namely the function $\widetilde{u}(x)$. As a consequence, $\widetilde{u}(x)$ is bound to be a black box that combines and reflects all possible psychological factors that affect the decision maker's preferences between lotteries. As discussed in Section 7, theories of decision-making alternative to EU, such as prospect theory, attempt to open the black box and disentangle these factors by adding additional free variables to the EU model.

5.7 Cardinal and Ordinal Utility, Reloaded

5.7.1 No Way Back

The realization that the five EU axioms are ordinal in nature, and that the cardinal utility function $\widetilde{u}(x)$ cannot be interpreted as equivalent to the utility function representing the decision maker's preferences between riskless options, convinced Friedman, Samuelson, Savage, and most of the economists of the 1950s that accepting von Neumann and Morgenstern's EU does not imply abandoning the ordinal approach, nor returning to a pre-Paretian conception of utility as a cardinally measurable entity.

5.7.2 A Novel Understating of Measurement

More generally, the debate on the nature of the von Neumann–Morgenstern utility function $\widetilde{u}(x)$ led Friedman and other economists to reconceptualize the notion of utility measurement in operational terms and, accordingly, to reconceptualize the meaning and relationships between ordinal and cardinal utility (see, e.g., Friedman & Savage 1952).

According to the novel operational view, measuring utility consists of assigning numbers to objects – be they riskless commodity bundles, lotteries, or the uncertain outcomes of lotteries – by following a definite set of operations. These numbers are called utility numbers or, more briefly, utilities. The way of assigning numbers to objects is largely arbitrary and conventional. The essential restriction is that the assigned utility numbers should allow the economist to predict the choice behavior of individuals. In particular, the numbers that the von Neumann–Morgenstern utility function $\widetilde{u}(x)$ assigns to the outcomes of lotteries are valid insofar as they allow the economist to predict which lottery the individual will choose.

5.7.3 A Happy Cohabitation

Within this prediction-oriented view of utility measurement advocated by Friedman and others, the contrast between ordinal and cardinal utility fades away. From this viewpoint, in fact, it is no longer the case that utility is intrinsically cardinal or intrinsically (just) ordinal. Rather, ordinal and cardinal utility indicate two equally legitimate ways of assigning numbers to the objects of choice. Accordingly, in areas of economic analysis where ordinal utility suffices to obtain valuable results, such as demand analysis and the theory of market equilibrium, only ordinal utility is needed. In other areas of economic analysis, such as the theory of choice under risk or the theory of decisions over time, where manageable models and valuable results need cardinal utility, cardinal utility can be legitimately adopted.

The view of utility measurement advocated by Friedman and others quickly became standard among mainstream utility theorists. Its success goes far toward explaining the peaceful cohabitation of cardinal and ordinal utility within utility analysis that began in the mid-1950s and has continued to the present day.

5.8 The As-If Interpretation of EU

In Section 5.5, we mentioned the as-if interpretation of EU originally advanced by Friedman and Savage (1948) and refined by Friedman (1953). In this latter work, Friedman argued that the relevant criterion by which to judge the scientific value of an economic theory is not the realism of its assumptions but its ability to yield accurate predictions:

> The relevant question to ask about the "assumptions" of a theory is not whether they are descriptively "realistic," for they never are, but whether they are sufficiently good approximations for the purpose in hand. And this question can be answered only by seeing whether the theory works, which means whether it yields sufficiently accurate predictions. (Friedman 1953, 15)

If, despite the patent unrealism of its assumptions, a theory yields accurate predictions for a certain class of economic phenomena, one can say that those phenomena work *as if* the assumptions of the theory were realistic.

When applied to EU and possibly other economic models of decision-making, the as-if view states that these models should account for the observable choices that individuals make, without pretending to capture the underlying psychological mechanisms that might generate those choices. Some underlying choice-generating mechanism – such as the multiply-and-add mechanism of Bernoulli's EU or the preference-based mechanism of von Neumann and Morgenstern EU – is attached to the model. However, in the as-if approach, the decision theorist is agnostic about whether this mechanism actually operates in the mind of the decision maker. The decision theorist may even deem, and explicitly acknowledge, that the posited mechanism and its components are only fictional constructs. Nonetheless, he explains, describes, or predicts the decision maker's choices *as if* they were generated by the underlying psychological mechanism at issue. Insofar as the as-if model is capable of accounting for the decision maker's choice behavior, the model is considered scientifically valid.

Since the early 1950s, Friedman's as-if methodology and, more specifically, the as-if interpretation of EU has been very popular among mainstream economists. In Section 7, we will see that the search for decision models that could be alternatives to EU was accompanied, at least in certain quarters, by the rejection of the as-if methodology.

5.9 The Status of the Components of von Neumann and Morgenstern's EU

In Section 2.7.4, we observed that Bernoulli appears to believe that the utility of money, and the circumstance that the marginal utility of money decreases as the person's wealth increases, are actually existing features of people's minds.

In Section 3.3.1, we saw that during the ordinal turn the primary notion of economic analysis ceased to be the notion of utility and became the notion of preference. More precisely, the ordinalists of the 1930s and 1940s deemed that individuals harbor in their minds well-behaved preferences between commodity bundles, and saw the utility function as a theoretical construct that represents preferences numerically. For them, however, the utility function might not have any real psychological correlate in the individual's mind. To use a formula, we can say that the ordinalists were realist (aka mentalist) about preferences but antirealist (aka instrumentalist or constructivist) about the utility function representing preferences (for a discussion of the ordinalists' position on these issues, see Moscati 2018, chaps. 5–7).

Moving to EU, it is fair to say that the majority of decision theorists who since the early 1950s have accepted EU maintain an approach similar to that of the ordinalists of the 1930s and 1940s, namely they are realist about risk preferences and antirealist about the von Neumann–Morgenstern utility function $\widetilde{u}(x)$ used to represent risk preferences. In other words, most decision theorists advocating EU appear to deem that decision makers harbor in their minds well-behaved preferences between lotteries and that these preferences allow them to rank the available lotteries and choose the most preferred one. In contrast, the function $\widetilde{u}(x)$ is conceived of as a theoretical construct that makes it possible to explain, describe, or predict the behavior of a decision maker under conditions of risk but that may not have any psychological correlate in the decision maker's mind (see, e.g., Luce & Raiffa 1957, 31–32; Binmore 2009, 19–20).

As I have argued more extensively elsewhere (Moscati in press), I find it questionable to conceive of risk preferences à la von Neumann–Morgenstern as psychologically realistic entities. In fact, these preferences are not the preferences of commonsense or folk-psychology but formal objects – more precisely, binary relations – that are supposed to satisfy a set of demanding properties, such as completeness, transitivity, and stability across choice domains and elicitation methods. As discussed in Section 5.4, it is, however, dubious that actual decision makers harbor in their minds complete, transitive, and stable preferences. Accordingly, I submit, the risk preferences featured in von Neumann and Morgenstern's EU as well as the preference-based decision mechanism relying on them (see Section 5.1.2) should be interpreted just like the utility function $\widetilde{u}(x)$, that is, as theoretical constructs through which decision theorists attempt to describe or predict the behavior of decision makers under risk but that may not have any psychological correlate in the minds of decision makers.

6 Savage's EU

Bernoulli's EU and von Neumann–Morgenstern's EU are models for decision-making under conditions of risk, that is, for situations where the objective probabilities of alternative events are available and decision makers know them. However, several decisions are made under conditions of uncertainty where objective probabilities are not available or are not known by the decision maker. Think, for instance, of a patient who decides whether to undergo surgery, or an investor who decides which financial asset to buy.

Building on the work of Frank Ramsey ([1926] 1931) and Bruno de Finetti ([1937] 1980), in his book *The Foundations of Statistics* Savage ([1954] 1972) showed how subjective probabilities can be defined and, based on them, how EU can be extended to situations of uncertainty.

6.1 Two Approaches, One Definition

When we abandon objective probabilities, two distinct approaches to developing a theory of decision-making under uncertainty as well as a theory of subjective or personal probability can be adopted, namely the intuitive-probability approach and the preference-based approach. Although the approach that dominates decision analysis and that was adopted by Savage is the preference-based approach, we will briefly discuss the intuitive-probability approach too.

Despite their differences, the two approaches to subjective probability agree on the definition of what a probability measure $p(E)$ is. This is the axiomatic definition of probability provided by Kolmogorov (1933) and accepted by most probability theorists. According to this definition, a probability measure is a real-valued function $p(E)$ over a suitable set of events that satisfies the following three properties: (1) the number $p(E_i)$ assigned to any event E_i must fall in the range $[0, 1]$: $0 \leq p(E_i) \leq 1$; (2) the probability number assigned to the certain event Ω is 1: $p(\Omega) = 1$; (3) if E_i and E_j are mutually exclusive events, the probability of the event obtained by their union is equal to the sum of the probabilities of E_i and E_j: if $E_i \cap E_j = \emptyset$, then $p(E_i \cup E_j) = p(E_i) + p(E_j)$.

6.2 The Intuitive-Probability Approach

The intuitive-probability approach, or introspective approach, or direct approach to subjective probability, was developed by, among others, Koopman (1940), Kraft, Pratt, and Seidenberg (1959), Shafer (1981), Chateauneuf (1985), Karni (1996), and others. In this this line of research, the individual's beliefs are the primitive element of the analysis: It is assumed that the individual has beliefs about the relative likelihood of events before and independently of her preferences or choices between alternative courses of action and that she can access these beliefs by introspection.

More precisely, beliefs are modeled as binary order relations that, rather than ranking commodities, lotteries, or courses of action, rank events. By analogy with the preference relation $\succcurlyeq$, we can indicate the belief relation with the symbol $\overset{..}{\succcurlyeq}$, so that $E_1 \overset{..}{\succcurlyeq} E_2$ means that the individual believes that event E_1 is at least as likely as event E_2. If the belief relation $\overset{..}{\succcurlyeq}$ is complete and transitive, it is called a "qualitative probability."

If certain additional conditions are satisfied (see Kraft, Pratt, and Seidenberg 1959), the belief relation $\overset{..}{\succcurlyeq}$ can be represented numerically by a belief function $b(E)$, just like the preference relation $\succcurlyeq$ can be represented numerically by a utility function $u(x)$. As in the case of the preference relation $\succcurlyeq$, saying that $b(E)$ represents $\overset{..}{\succcurlyeq}$ means that $E_1 \overset{..}{\succcurlyeq} E_2$ if and only if $b(E_1) \geq b(E_2)$.

The function $b(E)$ just expresses how the individual ranks events according to their perceived likelihood. Accordingly, if $b(E_1) = 0.8$ and $b(E_2) = 0.4$, this only means that the individual believes that E_1 is more likely than E_2, not that she believes that E_1 is twice as likely as E_2. This numerical example also clarifies that the belief function $b(E)$ is not yet a full-fledged, quantitative probability measure $p(E)$.

In order to guarantee that the belief function $b(E)$ is a probability measure $p(E)$ in the sense of Kolmogorov, the belief relation $\overset{..}{\succcurlyeq}$ should satisfy some further and rather technical conditions (see Chateauneuf 1985). If these conditions are met, it is possible to assign to each of the uncertain events $E_1, \ldots, E_N$ a number $p(E_i)$ that possesses the three characteristics stated by Kolmogorov and that can therefore be interpreted as the subjective probability that the decision maker assigns to event E_i.

Based on the subjective probabilities $p(E_i)$, the course of action $[x_1, E_1; \ldots; x_N, E_N]$ can be seen as a lottery yielding outcome x_1 with probability $p(E_1)$, outcome x_2 with probability $p(E_2)$, and so on. We can thus return to use EU, either in Bernoulli's version or in von Neumann and Morgenstern's version, to model the decision maker's choice behavior under conditions of uncertainty.

6.3 The Preference-Based Approach

6.3.1 A Criticism of Intuitive Probabilities

Ramsey, de Finetti, and Savage shared anti-psychologistic methodological views and were therefore skeptical about the possibility of eliciting beliefs via introspection or interrogation.

On the one hand, they argued, identifying beliefs by introspection is more complicated than it appears at first sight (see, e.g., Savage [1954] 1972, 27). Moreover, even if the decision maker is capable of arriving at her own beliefs by introspection, it is far from obvious that, if interrogated with questions such as "which event do you believe is more likely?" she will answer truthfully or thoughtfully.

Second, the critics of the intuitive-probability approach observed that, even if the decision maker answers questions concerning her introspective belief truthfully and carefully, the relationship between these beliefs and her actual choice behavior may be problematic. If, on the one hand, the decision maker's introspective beliefs do not affect her actual choice behavior, eliciting them by introspection or interrogation would be irrelevant for decision analysis. If, in contrast, the decision maker's introspective beliefs do affect her choice behavior, then they could be elicited backwards, that is, by identifying what beliefs about the relative likelihood of events could have generated her choice behavior. To better illustrate this point, it is useful to quote Savage at some length:

> Even if the concept ["more probable to me than"] were so completely intuitive, which might justify direct interrogation . . ., what could such interrogation have to do with the behavior of a person in the face of uncertainty, except of course for his verbal behavior under interrogation? If the state of mind in question is not capable of manifesting itself in some sort of extraverbal behavior, it is extraneous to our main interest. If, on the other hand, it does manifest itself through more material behavior, that should, at least in principle, imply the possibility of testing whether a person holds one event to be more probable than another, by some behavior expressing, and giving meaning to, his judgment. (Savage 1954 [1972], 27–28)

The idea of eliciting beliefs indirectly from preferences or choices, rather than directly from introspection, is what characterizes the preference-based, or choice-theoretic, or indirect approach to belief elicitation. This approach was pioneered by Ramsey and de Finetti in the 1920s and 1930s, advanced by Savage in the 1950s, and developed in subsequent years by various scholars, notably Anscombe and Aumann (1963).

6.3.2 How the Preference-Based Approach Works

The key problem with the preference-based approach to belief elicitation is that, as mentioned in Section 5.6.2, the decision maker's preferences between alternative courses of action do not depend only on her beliefs about the likelihood of events but also on other factors, such as her preference between the outcomes, her attitude toward risk, or the pleasure or displeasure she may associate with the very act of gambling. The elicitation of beliefs from preferences or choice behavior should therefore guarantee that the influence of these additional and confounding factors is somehow neutralized.

To have an idea about how this can be done and, more generally, about how beliefs can be elicited from preferences or choices, imagine a situation where there are only two possible events, E_1 and E_2, and two bets, A_1 and A_2. Bet A_1 yields \$100 if event E_1 occurs, and \$0 if event E_2 occurs: $A_1 = [\$100, E_1; \$0, E_2]$. Bet A_2 is symmetrical to A_1, in the sense that it yields \$0 if event E_1 occurs, and \$100 if event E_2 occurs: $A_2 = [\$0, E_1; \$100, E_2]$.

Under the plausible assumption that the decision maker prefers more money to less money, if she prefers and chooses A_1 it seems reasonable to infer from her preference that she judges event E_1 more likely than event E_2. Conversely, if the decision maker prefers A_2, we can infer that for her E_2 is more likely than E_1.

In other words, the preference relation $\succcurlyeq$ that ranks bets A_1 and A_2 allows us to define a belief relation $\overset{..}{\succcurlyeq}$ that ranks events E_1 and E_2 according to their relative likelihood: $E_1 \overset{..}{\succcurlyeq} E_2$ if and only if $A_1 \succcurlyeq A_2$. The difference with respect to the intuitive-probability approach is that, in it, the belief ranking $\overset{..}{\succcurlyeq}$ was the primitive element of the analysis and was identified by introspection; here, the belief relation $\overset{..}{\succcurlyeq}$ is derived from the preference relation $\succcurlyeq$. One may argue that this difference is too subtle or too technical to have any relevant consequence. In Section 6.7, however, we will consider an example showing that this is not the case.

Returning to the preference-based approach, the ranking of events expressed by $\overset{..}{\succcurlyeq}$ is at most a qualitative probability. To transform it into something that can be represented by a full-fledged probability measure $p(E)$, a series of conditions should be satisfied. In Section 6.4, we will discuss what these conditions are.

For the moment, it is important to point out that when we elicit the decision maker's belief ranking from her preference ranking of bets like $A_1 = [\$100, E_1; \$0, E_2]$ and $A_2 = [\$0, E_1; \$100, E_2]$, it seems sufficiently safe to assume that a series of potential confounding factors have been neutralized. In fact, since the possible outcomes of the two bets are the same (\$0 and \$100), the preferences between the outcomes, whatever they are, cancel out and therefore should not influence the way the decision maker ranks A_1 and A_2. Moreover, since the two uncertain events are also the same (E_1 and E_2), even the decision maker's attitude toward risk should not influence the way she ranks bets A_1 and A_2. Finally, since the bets have an identical structure, the pleasure or displeasure the decision maker might associate with the very act of gambling should affect the bets in the same manner, and therefore, again, should not influence her ranking of A_1 and A_2.

In his *Foundations of Statistics*, Savage used a preference-based approach similar to the one just described to define subjective probabilities and thus to extend von Neumann and Morgenstern's EU to situations where objective probabilities are not available. Therefore, his theory, which has been labeled "the crowning glory of choice theory" (Kreps 1988, 120), is called subjective EU. We now examine it in more detail.[8]

6.4 Savage's Axioms

The domain of objects Savage's theory refers to are possible courses of action of the form $[x_1, E_1; \ldots; x_N, E_N]$. Savage called the courses of action "acts" and their possible outcomes $x_1, \ldots, x_N$ "consequences." When the outcomes of an act are amounts of money, Savage called it a "bet." A course of action or bet i will be indicated as A_i.

Following von Neumann and Morgenstern's approach, Savage assumed that the decision maker can rank acts available to her according to a binary relation $\succeq$ that is interpreted as a preference relation. The preference must satisfy seven axioms or postulates that Savage ([1954] 1972, 7) indicated as P1–P7 and to which he gave a normative interpretation as maxims of rational behavior: "I am about to build up a highly idealized theory of the behavior of a 'rational' person with respect to decisions. In doing so I will . . . have to ask you to agree with me that such and such maxims of behavior are 'rational'." Even more explicitly, in another passage of the *Foundations* Savage added: "The main use I would make of P1 and its successors is normative, to police my own decisions for consistency" (20).

I will illustrate Savage's seven postulates more quickly and less formally than I did in Section 4 for von Neumann and Morgenstern's axioms. For more detailed and technical treatments, see Savage ([1954] 1972), Kreps (1988), and Gilboa (2009).

6.4.1 P1

P1 requires (no surprise) that the preference relation $\succeq$ between acts is complete and transitive.

In Section 5.3.3, we saw that Aumann (1962) and others argued that assuming that decision makers have complete preferences between lotteries, that is, between risky options for which the probabilities of outcomes are known, is problematic from both a descriptive and a normative viewpoint. Several decision theorists have contended that assuming that decision makers have complete

---

[8] An approach to subjective probability and individual decision-making alternative to Savage's approach has been proposed by Richard Jeffrey ([1965] 1990). In Jeffrey's theory, which has been more influential in philosophy than economics, the choice options are propositions, such as "I have a refreshing swim," and the desirability of an option is calculated by using the operations of propositional calculus. Despite the differences between Jeffrey's theory and EU, Jeffrey's formula for expressing the desirability of an option is structurally very similar to the EU formula. Broome (1990) offers a nice presentation of Jeffrey's theory.

preferences between uncertain options for which the probabilities of outcomes are not known is even more problematic. For instance, Gilboa, Postlewaite, and Schmeidler (2008, 180) remark:

> In the presence of uncertainty ... completeness of preferences is a less compelling assumption. Assume that Carol is taking a new job, and she is offered either one pension plan with defined benefits that depend in a complex way on wages and years of service, or a plan with defined contributions whose eventual pension payments will depend on the amount contributed, return on investment, and choices over types of payouts made at retirement. Carol is likely to have no a priori preferences between the plans.

6.4.2 P2

In the same spirit as the Independence Axiom (see Section 4.3.4), P2 requires that the preference ranking between two courses of action A_1 and A_2 does not depend on the parts where A_1 and A_2 agree but only on the parts where they differ. More formally, assume that with respect to a certain subset S of the events $E_1, \ldots, E_N$, the courses of action A_1 and A_2 yield different outcomes, while for all remaining events not included in S, they yield the same outcome. P2 requires that, if the decision maker prefers A_1 to A_2 when she compares them with respect to the events in S, she should also prefer A_1 to A_2 globally, that is, with respect to the entire space of events.

P2 expresses the key part of what Savage ([1954] 1972, 21–24) calls the Sure-Thing principle (see Section 5.3.1) and in the decision-theoretic literature the Sure-Thing principle is often identified with P2. However, Savage's original usage of the principle requires that P2 is supplemented by two other postulates, namely P3 and P7.

6.4.3 P3

P3 requires that the decision maker's preference ranking of outcomes does not depend on the event in which the outcomes are obtained. To see what P3 rules out, and why it can be problematic, consider the following situation, which builds on an example originally suggested by Aumann in a letter to Savage (Aumann [1971] 2000; see also Gilboa 2009, chaps. 10 and 12).

E_1 is the event "sunny weather," and E_2 is the event "rainy weather," x_1 is "having an umbrella," and x_2 is "having a swimsuit." The decision maker has to choose between $A_1 = $ [umbrella, sunny; umbrella, rainy] and $A_2 = $ [swimsuit, sunny; swimsuit, rainy], that is, between having with her the umbrella in any event or the swimsuit in any event. If the decision maker prefers A_1 to A_2, in Savage's framework this implies that she prefers having the umbrella to having the swimsuit: umbrella $\succ$ swimsuit. P3 requires that this preference ranking does not change if the event in which the umbrella or the swimsuit are obtained changes.

Therefore, if the decision maker comes to know that the event E_1 occurs for certain, that is, that it will be sunny, so that she has now to choose between $A_3 =$ [umbrella, sunny] and $A_4 =$ [swimsuit, sunny], P3 rules out that she prefers A_4 to A_3 because this would imply that now for her swimsuit $\succ$ umbrella, that is, a reversal of the previous preference ranking. However, from both a normative and a descriptive viewpoint, it seems perfectly fine to prefer A_1 to A_2 *and* A_4 to A_3.

In his reply to Aumann, Savage acknowledged the difficulty but suggested that it can be somehow overcome by an appropriate redefinition of the outcomes. However, this redefinition strategy is arguably problematic (for a discussion, see Gilboa 2009; Baccelli & Mongin 2022).

6.4.4 P4

P4 is fundamental to ensure that the preference-based approach to belief elicitation described in Section 6.3.2 works, and it can be seen as a complement to P3. Just as P3 requires that the decision maker's preference ranking of outcomes does not depend on the events used to infer the preference ranking, P4 requires that the decision maker's ranking of the likelihood of events does not depend on the outcomes used to infer the likelihood ranking.

To clarify what this means, let us return to the example used in Section 6.3.2 to illustrate the preference-based approach. In that example, the decision maker prefers $A_1 =$ [$100, E_1$; $0, E_2$] to $A_2 =$ [$0, E_1$; $100, E_2$], and from this preference ranking we infer that for him E_1 is more likely than E_2. Now imagine that the decision maker is faced with bet $A_3 =$ [$200, E_1$; $50, E_2$] and bet $A_4 =$ [$50, E_1$; $200, E_2$]. Here, the outcomes have changed, but their ranking has not, in the sense that $200 \succ 50 just as $100 \succ 0.

Based on the decision maker's preference of A_1 over A_2, and the inferred belief that for him E_1 is more likely than E_2, we expect that she prefers A_3 to A_4. P4 guarantees that this is the case, that is, it rules out the possibility that $A_4 \succ A_3$. In effect, if the decision maker preferred A_1 to A_2 and A_4 to A_3, it would be impossible to infer whether for him E_1 is more likely than E_2 or vice versa, and the preference-based approach to belief elicitation would collapse.

6.4.5 P5–P7

Postulates P5–P7 are technical postulates. P5 rules out that the decision maker is indifferent among all outcomes. If this were the case, for example if the decision makers were indifferent between, say, $0 and $100, from the fact that she prefers $A_1 = [\$100, E_1; \$0, E_2]$ to $A_2 = [\$0, E_1; \$100, E_2]$, we could not infer that for her E_1 is more likely than E_2. Like P4, therefore, P5 also plays a role in guaranteeing that the preference-based approach to belief elicitation works.

P6 and P7 can be seen as continuity conditions. P6 rules out the existence of super-good or super-bad outcomes that may generate abrupt reversals, that is, discontinuities, in the decision maker's preference ranking between courses of action. P7 states that if, with respect to a certain set of events, a course of action A_1 is preferred to each of the outcomes $x_1, \ldots, x_N$ of another course of action A_2, then, with respect to the same set of events, A_1 should be preferred to A_2. Thus P7 too rules out unexpected preference reversals.

6.5 Savage's Theorem and Its Interpretation

Savage's theorem is a representation theorem analogous to von Neumann and Morgenstern's. It states that if the decision maker's preferences satisfy postulates P1–P7, these preferences can be represented by a numerical function and that this function has the EU form.

6.5.1 Statement

More precisely, the theorem states that, if the decision maker's preference relation $\succcurlyeq$ between courses of action $[x_1, E_1; \ldots; x_N, E_N]$ satisfies axioms P1–P7, then:

(1) there exists a probability measure $p(E)$ defined over the set of the events $E_1, \ldots, E_N$;

(2) there exists a real-valued function $\widetilde{u}(x)$ defined over the set of the outcomes $x_1, \ldots, x_N$;

(3) for any two courses of action A_1 and A_2, the decision maker prefers A_1 to A_2 if and only if the mathematical expectation of A_1 is larger than the mathematical expectation of A_2, whereby mathematical expectations are calculated using the functions $p(E)$ and $\widetilde{u}(x)$; more succinctly, $A_1 \succcurlyeq A_2$ if and only if $\sum_{A_1} \widetilde{u}(x_i) p(E_i) \geq \sum_{A_2} \widetilde{u}(x_i) p(E_i)$. Furthermore,

(4) the probability measure $p(E)$ is unique;

(5) the real-valued function $\widetilde{u}(x)$ is unique up to linearly increasing transformations, that is, $\widetilde{u}(x)$ is cardinal in nature.

6.5.2 Interpretation

The probability measure $p(E)$ can be interpreted as expressing the subjective or personal probability that the decision maker attaches to each of the events $E_1, \ldots, E_N$. The uniqueness of $p(E)$ means that the decision maker's probability assignments are univocally determined, that is, it rules out the possibility that the decision maker attaches to an event E_i two different probabilities, that is, $p(E_i) = 0.7$ and $p(E_i) = 0.8$.

The function $\widetilde{u}(x)$ can be interpreted as a utility function, in the basic ordinalist sense that the decision maker prefers outcome x_1 to outcome x_2 if and only if $\widetilde{u}(x_1) \geq \widetilde{u}(x_2)$.

Accordingly, Savage's theorem can be interpreted as stating that, if postulates P1–P7 are satisfied, the decision maker prefers the course of action associated with the highest expected utility, whereby this expected utility is calculated by using the utility function $\widetilde{u}(x)$ and the subjective-probability measure $p(E)$.

6.5.3 Probability First

We are not going to examine the proof of Savage's theorem, but it is useful to have a rough idea of its structure.

First, Savage uses the preference-based approach to belief elicitation that we have outlined in Section 6.3.2 to define a belief relation $\succeq$ over pairs of events. Then he shows that axioms P1–P7 guarantee that the belief relation $\succeq$ so constructed can be represented by a unique probability measure $p(E)$ and that $p(E)$ can be extended and applied to situations where more than two events are possible. Finally, Savage shows that postulates P1–P7 warrant not only the existence of a unique probability measure $p(E)$ but also the existence of a utility function $\widetilde{u}(x)$, such that $A_1 \succeq A_2$ if and only if $\sum_{A_1} \widetilde{u}(x_i) p(E_i) \geq \sum_{A_2} \widetilde{u}(x_i) p(E_i)$.

The structure of Savage's proof is important because it makes clear that the identification of a probability measure $p(E)$ is a precondition for the construction of his subjective version of EU. In Sections 6.6 and 6.7, we will consider two choice situations in which, however, the elicitation of $p(E)$ from preferences between acts is problematic. The first situation is associated with the so-called Ellsberg paradox, while the second is associated with the case of so-called state-dependent preferences. Notably, in neither case the difficulty, or impossibility, of eliciting beliefs from preferences can be easily discarded on normative grounds, that is, by attributing it to some form of irrationality.

6.6 The Ellsberg Paradox

6.6.1 Ellsberg's Urn

Daniel Ellsberg (1961) presented the following choice situation that later became known as the Ellsberg paradox. He imagined an urn containing ninety balls, thirty of which are red. The remaining sixty balls are either black or yellow in some unknown proportion. One ball is to be drawn at random from the urn, and Ellsberg considered two pairs of bets on the color of the ball.

In the first pair of bets, bet A_1 yields \$100 if the drawn ball is red, and \$0 if it is black or yellow, while bet A_2 yields \$0 if the ball is red or yellow, and \$100 if it is black: $A_1 = [\$100, \text{red}; \$0, \text{black or yellow}]$ and $A_2 = [\$0, \text{red or yellow}; \$100, \text{black}]$. Ellsberg argued that most people would prefer bet A_1 to bet A_2: $A_1 \succ A_2$. He also asked a group of eminent decision theorists to state their preferences, and many of them, including Marschak and Savage, preferred A_1 to A_2.

In the second pair of bets, bet A_3 yields \$100 if the ball is red or yellow, and \$0 if it is black, while A_4 yields \$0 if the ball is red, and \$100 if it is black or yellow: $A_3 = [\$100, \text{red or yellow}; \$0, \text{black}]$ and $A_4 = [\$0, \text{red}; \$100, \text{black or yellow}]$. Ellsberg argued that in this situation most people would prefer A_4 to A_3, and he noted that Marschak and Savage also preferred A_4 to A_3.

To see why these two preference rankings are problematic, note that if we adopt the preference-based approach to belief elicitation discussed in the previous sections, $A_1 \succ A_2$ indicates that the decision maker considers event $E_1 = $ "the ball is red" more likely than event $E_2 = $ "the ball is black": if $A_1 \succ A_2$, then $p(E_1) > p(E_2)$. Similarly, $A_4 \succ A_3$ indicates that the decision maker considers event $E_4 = $ "the ball is black or yellow" more likely than event $E_3 = $ "the ball is red or yellow": if $A_4 \succ A_3$, then $p(E_4) > p(E_3)$.

Now, since the events "the ball is black" and "the ball is yellow" are mutually exclusive, the probability $p(E_4)$ that the ball is either black or yellow is equal to the sum of the probability $p(E_2)$ that the ball is black and the probability $p(E_5)$ that the ball is yellow: $p(E_4) = p(E_2) + p(E_5)$. Similarly, the probability $p(E_3)$ that the ball is either red or yellow is equal to the sum of the probability $p(E_1)$ that the ball is red and the probability $p(E_5)$ that the ball is yellow: $p(E_3) = p(E_1) + p(E_5)$. If we substitute these sums into the inequality $p(E_4) > p(E_3)$, we obtain $p(E_2) + p(E_5) > p(E_1) + p(E_5)$, that is, $p(E_2) > p(E_1)$.

Therefore, the fact that the decision maker prefers A_4 to A_3 seems to indicate that for her $p(E_2) > p(E_1)$, that is, that she believes that "black" is more likely than "red." Her preferring A_1 to A_2, in contrast, seems to indicate that for her $p(E_1) > p(E_2)$, that is, that she considers "red" more likely than "black." For Ellsberg (1961, 655), however, this contrast does not show that the decision maker holds incompatible beliefs but only that sometimes it is impossible to infer beliefs from preferences and, consequently, to describe choices between alternative courses of action through the EU model:

It is impossible, on the basis of such choices, to infer even qualitative probabilities for the events in question . . ... Moreover, for any values of the pay-offs, it is impossible to find probability numbers in terms of which these choices could be described – even roughly or approximately – as maximizing the mathematical expectation of utility.

6.6.2 Normativity Issues and Ambiguity Aversion

In his article, Ellsberg showed that the preference pattern $A_1 \succ A_2$ and $A_4 \succ A_3$ violates Savage's axiom P2. However, he argued, such a preference pattern and the violation of P2 cannot be discarded on normative grounds. Ellsberg made his case in two steps.

First, he noted that some of the eminent decision theorists he had approached, including Marschak and even Savage, not only preferred A_1 to A_2 and A_4 to A_3 but wished to maintain these preferences even once they understood that these preferences violate P2. Ellsberg remarked that it would be difficult to label these decision theorists as irrational persons.

Secondly, Ellsberg suggested a psychological explanation of why people typically prefer A_1 to A_2 and A_4 to A_3, namely their aversion to what he called "ambiguity." According to Ellsberg, for a decision maker an uncertain situation is ambiguous when the information she has for evaluating the relative likelihood of alternative events is poor, so that she is not very confident about her own likelihood judgments.

In the case of the urn, the decision maker knows without ambiguity that 30 balls, or $\frac{1}{3}$ of the 90 balls in the urn, are red, and that 60, or $\frac{2}{3}$, are either black or yellow. The ambiguous information concerns the amount of black and yellow balls, which can be anything between 0 and 60, that is, any fraction between 0 and $\frac{2}{3}$.

This ambiguity, or lack thereof, reflects on the four bets A_1, A_2, A_3, and A_4. Bets A_1 and A_4 are not ambiguous. Actually, they are lotteries with objective probabilities: A_1 yields \$100 with probability $\frac{1}{3}$, and \$0 with probability $\frac{2}{3}$, while A_4 yields \$100 with probability $\frac{2}{3}$, and \$0 with probability $\frac{1}{3}$. In contrast, A_2 and A_3 are ambiguous because they both refer to the events "red or yellow" and "black," whose probabilities can be anything between, respectively, $\frac{1}{3}$ and 1 and 0 and $\frac{2}{3}$.

Now, Ellsberg hypothesizes that decision makers do not like ambiguity, that is, that they do not like to bet upon events whose likelihood they are not confident about and that this is the reason why they prefer A_1 to A_2 and A_4 to A_3. Ellsberg adds that Savage's axioms, and notably axiom P2, implicitly rule out ambiguity aversion, although there are no compelling normative reasons to do so.

At any rate, in the early 1960s decision theorists tended to dismiss choice patterns à la Ellsberg either as errors that upon reflection decision makers would want to correct or as related to fictional and idiosyncratic choice situations.

6.7 State-Dependent Preferences

The second notable case in which the preference-based approach to belief elicitation is questionable is the one in which the decision maker's preferences are not uniform across all possible events but change from one event to another. These preferences are called "state-dependent preferences" and the utility function that represents them is called a "state-dependent utility function."

The problem was originally raised by Aumann in the letter to Savage that we already mentioned in Section 6.4.3 (Aumann [1971] 2000) and has been investigated, among others, by Karni and coauthors (for reviews of the literature, see Karni 2008; Baccelli 2021).

6.7.1 The Loving Husband's Bet

In his letter, Aumann imagined a man who loves his wife and feels that, without her, his life would become less worth living. The wife, however, is severely ill and to survive she has to undergo a difficult operation. The medical record of the operation shows that one-half of the patients survive the operation and are then completely cured (call this event E_1) while the remaining one-half of the patients die during the operation (call this event E_2). The husband is fully aware of this medical record, so it seems reasonable to assume that he attaches a subjective probability $\frac{1}{2}$ to each of the two events.

In a somehow rude way, the poor husband is now asked to state his preferences between the following two bets: bet A_1 yields $100 in the event E_1 that the wife survives and $0 in the event E_2 that the wife dies; the specular bet A_2 yields $0 if the wife survives and $100 if the wife dies: $A_1 = [\$100, \ E_1; \ \$0, \ E_2]$ and $A_2 = [\$0, \ E_1; \ \$100, \ E_2]$. Aumann observes that it is reasonable to assume that the husband would prefer to bet on his wife's survival, that is, for him $A_1 \succ A_2$.

The reason is that, if his wife dies, $100 would not mean much to him, while if his wife survives he would enjoy the $100, for example by celebrating together with his wife her recovery. The husband's motivation for preferring A_1 to A_2 appears well defendable on normative grounds.

The problem is that, if we apply the preference-based method to elicit belief introduced in Section 6.3.2 and discussed throughout this section, from the circumstance that the husband prefers A_1 to A_2 we have to infer that for him $p(E_1) > p(E_2)$, while in fact we know that he attaches probability $\frac{1}{2}$ to both events.

6.7.2 Variations of the Story

In the literature on state-dependent preferences, different versions of the loving-husband story, with different decision-theoretic implications, have been proposed (for a philosophically oriented overview, see Baccelli 2017). In some versions, the husband's state-dependent preferences involve a violation of some of Savage's axioms, typically P4 but sometimes P3. In other versions, the husband's preferences satisfy all of Savage's axioms, but they can be represented by a multiplicity of probability measures (each in combination with an appropriate utility function) rather than by a unique probability measure. In this case, the probability he attaches to the event that his wife survives the operation can be, say, either 0.3 or 0.7, which makes it difficult to interpret these numbers as representing the husband's degrees of beliefs: Does he believe that his wife will survive with a probability 0.7 or only with a probability 0.3?

In the version of the story considered above, where the medical record induces the husband to attach probability $\frac{1}{2}$ to each of the two events, the situation is still different. Even if it is possible to elicit unique values $p(E_1)$ and $p(E_2)$, with $p(E_1) > p(E_2)$, from the husband's preferences between A_1 and A_2, it is still hard to interpret these values as indicating his beliefs because we know that he judges the two events as equally likely. Imagine, for instance, that the wife is uncertain about whether or not to undergo the operation and asks her husband about the likelihood of a successful operation. It is reasonable to imagine that the loving but sincere husband will answer "one-half" rather than "more than one-half."

To sum up the discussion, as in the case of the Ellsberg paradox, in the case of preferences that are state-dependent the preference-based method to elicit beliefs from preferences is also problematic. A number of solutions to this problem have been proposed, one of which would be to complement the preference-based approach to belief elicitation with the intuitive-probability approach discussed in Section 6.2. However, this line of attack also presents some problems and has not gained general acceptance (for overviews and discussion, see again Karni 2008; Baccelli 2021).

6.8 The Status of the Components of Savage's EU

Concerning the theoretical status of the components of Savage's EU – namely, the preference relation $\succeq$ between courses of actions, the utility function $\tilde{u}(x)$, and the probability measure $p(E)$ – we can roughly repeat what we said in Section 5.9 with reference to the status of the components of von Neumann and Morgenstern's EU. That is, Savage and the majority of decision theorists who accept his subjective version of EU are realist about the preference relation $\succeq$, in the sense that they assume that individuals do harbor in their minds well-behaved preferences between courses of actions, but antirealist about the utility function $\widetilde{u}(x)$ and the probability measure $p(E)$, in the sense that the latter are conceived as theoretical constructs that may not have any psychological correlate in the individuals' mind (for a discussion, see Zynda 2000).

In the paper already mentioned in Section 5.9, namely Moscati (in press), I have argued that even the preference relation $\succcurlyeq$ featured in Savage's EU is best understood as a theoretical construct that does not have a psychological correlate in the mind of decision makers, and this because it is dubious that actual decision makers harbor in their minds complete and transitive preferences between courses of action.

7 Beyond EU: Prospect Theory

Until the mid-1960s, most decision theorists tended to dismiss violations of EU along the choice patterns imagined by Allais and Ellsberg either as errors that upon reflection decision makers would want to correct or as related to fictional choice situations that rarely occur in reality. In the mid-1960s, however, things began to change.

A series of laboratory experiments showed that choice patterns à la Allais and Ellsberg are in fact frequent and predictable and that most decision makers do not consider them as mistakes and are not willing to correct them (for reviews of this experimental work, see Schoemaker 1982; Moscati 2018). From the late 1960s to the early 1970s, other decision patterns violating EU were highlighted by a group of young psychologists based at the University of Michigan, namely Sarah Lichtenstein, Paul Slovic, and Amos Tversky (see, e.g., Tversky 1969; Lichtenstein & Slovic 1971). Beginning in the mid-1970s, a number of models aimed at accommodating decision patterns that EU cannot account for, such as Handa's (1977) certainty equivalence model and Kahneman and Tversky's (1979) prospect theory, were put forward. The flux of decision models proposed as alternatives to EU has continued until today.

Among the decision models for decisions under risk put forward since 1980, here we can mention rank-dependent utility theory, regret theory, various models featuring disappointment, cumulative prospect theory, the priority heuristic model, and salience theory. Among the models of decision-making in situations of uncertainty, extensions or modifications of Savage's EU include Choquet expected utility, cumulative prospect theory for uncertainty, maximin expected utility, and the smooth model of ambiguity (for reviews of this literature, see Schoemaker 1982; Starmer 2000; Gilboa 2009; Wakker 2010; Lipman & Pesendorfer 2013; Bordalo, Gennaioli, & Shleifer 2022).

In effect, none of these decision models has yet achieved the level of consensus that EU once enjoyed. In 2013, in concluding their comprehensive survey of the decision-theoretic literature, Gilboa and Marinacci (2013, 232) argued that it is not clear that a single theory of decision-making under risk or uncertainty will replace EU and that, "even if a single paradigm will eventually emerge, it is probably too soon to tell which one it will be." It is fair to say that the state of the art in decision theory has not changed over the last ten years.

That said, among the models for decision-making under risk and uncertainty mentioned above the most influential ones arguably are the original version of prospect theory (Kahneman & Tversky 1979; henceforth, OPT) and its modified version cumulative prospect theory (Tversky & Kahneman 1992; henceforth, CPT). To provide a hint about the post-EU theories of decision-making, the manner in which they overcome the problems of EU, the way they explain risk attitudes differently from EU, and the problems they present, here I focus on OPT and CPT. As discussed in Section 7.1.6, OPT presents some drawbacks that CPT attempts to overcome. However, it is useful to start with OPT because it allows a relatively simple introduction to notions and ideas that CPT elaborates.

7.1 Prospect Theory, Original Version

The original version of prospect theory is best understood as an extension of Bernoulli's utility-based EU, rather than von Neumann and Morgenstern's preference-based EU. In the appendix to their 1979 article, Kahneman and Tversky sketch a preference-based, axiomatized version of OPT, which, however, does not play any significant role in their exposition of the theory. The basic components of OPT are a "value function," $v(y)$, and a "weighting function," $w(p)$.

7.1.1 The Value Function $v(y)$

The value function $v(y)$ is analogous to the Bernoullian utility function $u(x)$: it expresses the subjective valuation that the decision maker attaches to riskless outcomes and is cardinal in nature. However, it has some specific features that distinguish it from $u(x)$. For the sake of simplicity, in illustrating these features I focus on the case in which outcomes are amounts of money.

First, Kahneman and Tversky (1979, 277–278) argue that the basic principles of perception and judgment indicate that individuals normally perceive outcomes as gains or losses with respect to some reference point, rather than, as assumed in EU, as final states of wealth. If we indicate with r the decision maker's reference point, and with x the actual monetary payoff, for Kahneman and Tversky the value function $v(y)$ applies to outcomes defined as $y = x - r$.

For instance, if the decision maker's reference point is his initial wealth and he does not expect to gain anything, $r = \$0$, and the actual monetary payoff x coincides with the perceived outcome y: "I do not expect to gain anything; therefore if I obtain \$100, my gain is \$100." But the reference point could be an expected payoff, say, of \$150. In this case, an actual gain of \$100 is perceived as a loss: "I expect to gain \$150; thus if I obtain \$100, I feel as if I lose \$50." Here, $y = \$100 - \$150 = -\$50$. Alternatively, the reference point could be the average payoff. If, for example, everybody else, on average, has lost \$170, an actual loss of \$100 may be perceived as a gain: "On average, everybody else lost \$170; I lost only \$100 and thus I feel as if I gained \$70." Here, $y = -\$100 - (-\$170) = \$70$.

Second, for Kahneman and Tversky (279) psychological evidence also suggests that losses loom larger than equally sized gains, a feature that is called "loss aversion." Thus, for instance, for the decision maker the pain associated with a loss of \$100 is more severe, in absolute value, than the joy associated with a gain of \$100: $|v(-\$100)| > |v(+\$100)|$. At the formal level, loss aversion implies that the value function for losses is steeper than it is for gains. For instance, it could be that $v(y) = y$ for gains and $v(y) = 2y$ for losses.

Third, for Kahneman and Tversky the marginal subjective value of both gains and losses diminishes with their magnitude. This implies that for gains the value function $v(y)$ is concave, and in this it is similar to Bernoulli's utility function $u(x)$. For losses, the assumption of diminishing marginal value implies that $v(y)$ is convex.

7.1.2 The Weighting Function $w(p)$

While in Bernoulli's EU the utility $u(x)$ of an outcome is weighted, via multiplication, by its objective probability p, Kahneman and Tversky (1979, 280–283) argue that in effect individuals weight the subjective value $v(y)$ of an outcome by a "decision weight" $w(p)$ that depends on the objective probability p of obtaining the outcome but can be, and often is, different from p. For instance, if $p = 0.5$ and $w(p) = 0.6$, the decision maker overrates the objective probability p by assigning it a decision weight $w(p)$ that is larger than p. If, on the contrary, $p = 0.5$ and $w(p) = 0.4$, the decision maker underrates the objective probability p.

The function $w(p)$ expressing decision weights is called a "weighting function," and Kahneman and Tversky discuss a number of features that this function appears to display. In particular, they argue that individuals tend to overweight small probabilities, that is, $w(p) > p$ for small p, and to underweight large probabilities, that is, $w(p) < p$ for large p. Various functional forms that have these two features have been proposed. One of the most popular is that advanced by Prelec (1998), according to which $w(p) = \exp(-\beta(-\ln p)^\alpha)$, where α and β are two parameters such that $0 < \alpha < 1$ and $\beta > 0$; note that for $\alpha = \beta = 1$, $w(p) = p$.

Two comments on decision weights are in order. First, it is important to stress that Kahneman and Tversky's decision weights should not be confused with Savage's subjective probabilities (see Section 6). Savage's subjective probabilities are introduced to model situations where the decision maker does not know the objective probabilities of the outcomes, while Kahneman and Tversky's decision weights model situations where the decision maker knows the objective probabilities of the outcomes, and distorts them.

Second, while the features of the value function $v(y)$, namely reference-dependence, loss aversion, and concavity for gains/convexity for losses, do not seem to involve any apparent form of irrationality and therefore seem justifiable from a normative viewpoint, decision weights are normatively problematic. In fact, it is difficult to consider rational a decision maker who is supposed to know that the objective probability of a certain event is, say, $p = 0.5$, and who makes his decisions by attaching to that event a weight that is different from 0.5, say 0.4 or 0.6. In effect, Kahneman and Tversky put forward OPT as a model which is descriptively more adequate than EU but did not claim that OPT is normatively valid.

7.1.3 The OPT Formula

Now, according to original prospect theory the decision maker prefers the lottery associated with the highest value of the expression $\sum v(y_i)w(p_i)$.

The OPT formula has the same multiply-and-add structure of the EU formula $\sum u(x_i)p_i$. In both cases, an index expressing the subjective value that the decision maker assigns to an outcome is weighted, via multiplication, by a parameter representing the likelihood, actual or perceived, that he attaches to the event of obtaining that outcome. Then the weighted subjective values of the outcomes are added, and the resulting numerical value is taken as expressing the subjective value that the decision maker attributes to the whole lottery.

From a mathematical viewpoint, the main difference between the two formulas is that while in EU there is only one "free variable," namely $u(x)$, in OPT there are three of them: $v(y)$, r, and $w(p)$. In particular, if $v(y)$ is the same for gains and losses, $r = 0$, and $w(p) = p$, the EU formula and the OPT formula coincide. Therefore, EU can be seen a special case of OPT (or OPT can be seen as a generalization of EU). This means that, by construction, OPT can accommodate a set of choice patterns larger than EU. That is, choice patterns that violate EU, such as the one considered by Allais, can be accounted for by OPT. We illustrate how this can be done in Section 7.1.4.

From an interpretative viewpoint, the multiplicity of free variables in OPT makes it possible to "open the black box" (see Section 5.6.2), that is, to better distinguish the different psychological factors that may affect the decision maker's preferences between lotteries and that, in EU, are all conflated into $u(x)$. In particular, in Section 7.1.5 we will discuss how the three free variables of OPT can be mobilized to explain risk attitudes.

7.1.4 The Allais Paradox Reconsidered

To see how OPT can account for the Allais paradox, consider a decision maker whose reference point is the status quo, that is, $r = 0$, and for whom the value function is $v(y) = \sqrt{y}$. Since $v(y)$ is concave, for this decision maker the marginal value of payoffs is diminishing. For illustrative purposes, let us also assume that the weighting function of this decision maker has the functional form $w(p) = p^2$, which can be obtained from Prelec's functional form $w(p) = \exp(-\beta(-\ln p)^\alpha)$ (see Section 7.1.2) by putting $\alpha = 1$ and $\beta = 2$. Since $p^2 < p$ for all p between 0 and 1, this decision maker underrates not only large probabilities but also small probabilities. Thus, he attaches a decision weight of $w(p) = 0.81$ to probability $p = 0.9$ $(0.9^2 = 0.81)$, and a decision weight of $w(p) = 0.01$ to probability $p = 0.10$ $(0.1^2 = 0.01)$. The only objective probabilities this decision maker does not underrate are $p = 0$ and $p = 1$, since $0^2 = 0$ and $1^2 = 1$.

Recall that in the first stage of Allais' choice situation the decision maker prefers lottery $L_1 = [100{,}000{,}000, 1]$ to $L_2 = [500{,}000{,}000, \frac{10}{100}; 100{,}000{,}000, \frac{89}{100}; 0, \frac{1}{100}]$ (see Section 5.3.2). The OPT values of the two lotteries are, respectively, $OPT(L_1) = 1^2 \times \sqrt{100{,}000{,}000} = 10{,}000$ and $OPT(L_2) = 0.1^2 \times \sqrt{500{,}000{,}000} + 0.89^2 \times \sqrt{100{,}000{,}000} + 0.01^2 \times \sqrt{0} = 8{,}144.6$. Therefore, $OPT(L_1) > OPT(L_2)$ which mirrors the preference order $L_1 \succ L_2$.

In the second stage, the decision maker prefers $L_4 = [500{,}000{,}000, \frac{10}{100}; 0, \frac{90}{100}]$ to $L_3 = [100{,}000{,}000, \frac{11}{100}; 0, \frac{89}{100}]$. This preference order is also mirrored by the OPT values of the lotteries: $OPT(L_4) = 0.10^2 \times \sqrt{500{,}000{,}000} + 0.90^2 \times \sqrt{0} = 223{,}6$ and $OPT(L_3) = 0.11^2 \times \sqrt{100{,}000{,}000} + 0.89^2 \times \sqrt{0} = 121$. Therefore, OPT can account for the Allais pattern of choice, which ceases to be a paradox. Here, we have considered one specific combination of reference point r, value function

$v(y)$, and weighting function $w(p)$ that can do the job, but many other combinations of r, $v(y)$, and $w(p)$ would work.

7.1.5 Risk Attitudes within OPT

As discussed in Sections 2, 4, and 5, in EU the risk attitudes of decision makers are univocally associated with the curvature of the utility function, be it the Bernoulli function $u(x)$ or the von Neumann–Morgenstern function $\tilde{u}(x)$. In OPT, risk attitudes can be accounted for by two additional and independent factors: loss aversion and probability weighting. Here, we focus on the case of risk aversion (for a richer discussion, see O'Donoghue & Somerville 2018).

First, consider a decision maker for whom $r = 0$, and whose value function $v(y)$ is linear for both gains and losses. However, because of loss aversion, the linear value function for losses is steeper than it is for gains. For instance, $v(y) = y$ for gains and $v(y) = 2y$ for losses. Imagine also that this decision maker does not distort objective probabilities, so that for him decision weights $w(p)$ coincide with probabilities: $w(p) = p$.

With respect to lotteries involving both gain and losses, this decision maker displays risk aversion. Consider for example lottery $[-\$100, 0.5; \$150, 0.5]$, whose expected payoff is $0.5 \times (-\$100) + 0.5 \times \$150 = \$25$. The decision maker prefers receiving \$25 with certainty (OPT value equal to $1 \times 25 = 25$) to playing the lottery (OPT value equal to $0.5 \times 2(-100) + 0.5 \times 150 = -25$). Therefore, even if his value function is linear, with respect to this lottery the decision maker displays actuarially risk aversion, which draws entirely from his loss aversion.

Now, consider a lottery that involves only possible gains, so that loss aversion does not play any role, for example lottery $[\$50, 0.5; \$100, 0.5]$, whose expected payoff is $0.5 \times \$50 + 0.5 \times \$100 = \$75$. For the decision maker the reference point is still $r = 0$, his value function is still linear and equal to $v(y) = y$, but now he weights probabilities according to the weighting function $w(p) = p^2$. As already noted, since $p^2 < p$ for all p between 0 and 1, this decision maker systematically underrates the probabilities of outcomes and, in our example, the probability of gains \$50 and \$100. This decision maker prefers receiving \$75 with certainty (OPT value equal to is $1^2 \times 75 = 75$) to playing the lottery (OPT value equal to $0.5^2 \times 50 + 0.5^2 \times 100 = 37.5$), so he is risk-averse. In this case, however, his risk aversion draws entirely from the way he weights objective probabilities.

To complete the picture, it is useful to note that in OPT a decision maker may display risk aversion even if his value function $v(y)$ is convex, that is, even if for him, in the Bernoullian interpretation, the marginal utility of money is increasing. In the example we are considering, a decision maker whose value function is $v(y) = y^2$, while his weighting function is $w(p) = p^2$, prefers receiving \$75 with certainty (OPT value equal to $1^2 \times 75^2 = 5{,}625$) to playing the lottery (OPT value equal to $0.5^2 \times 50^2 + 0.5^2 \times 100^2 = 3{,}125$).

7.1.6 Criticisms of OPT

Two main criticisms have been raised against OPT, the first related to the source of its descriptive power and the second to its acceptability from a normative viewpoint.

As discussed in Section 7.1.3, the three free variables featured in OPT give it a descriptive power much larger than EU's in the sense that, by opportunely specifying the reference point r, the value function $v(y)$, and the weighting function $w(p)$, OPT can accommodate almost any observed choice pattern. For instance, in Section 7.1.4 we have seen how r, $v(y)$, and $w(p)$ can be specified to account for choice patterns à la Allais. According to some critics (see, e.g., Brandstätter, Gigerenzer, & Hertwig 2006), in OPT variable specification easily becomes an ad hoc exercise, which makes the theory practically unfalsifiable and therefore vacuous.

The second main criticism is that the type of decision weighting featured in OPT allows for violations of a principle that is considered normatively compelling for decision-making under risk, namely the principle of first-order stochastic dominance. Lottery L_1 is said to first-order stochastically dominate lottery L_2 if, for every outcome y, the probability of an outcome at least as good as y is higher in L_1 than in L_2 For brevity, in the following I skip the "first-order" phrase. For instance, lottery $L_1 = [\$50, 0.5; \$100, 0.5]$, which yields either \$50 or \$100, stochastically dominates lottery $L_2 = [\$40, 1]$, which always yields \$40. The principle of stochastic dominance states that if lottery L_1 stochastically dominates lottery L_2, the decision maker should prefer or choose L_1.

EU satisfies the principle of stochastic dominance, in the sense that if lottery L_1 stochastically dominates lottery L_2, the EU value of L_1 is always larger than the EU value of L_2. In contrast, as noted by many scholars (see, e.g., Fishburn 1978) OPT and other theories that feature OPT-like probability weighting allow for violation of stochastic dominance.

Consider, for instance, a decision maker for whom $r = 0$, $v(y) = y$, and $w(p) = p^2$. As already noted, this is a decision maker who systematically underrates the probabilities of outcomes, apart from $p = 0$ and $p = 1$. Accordingly, when he faces lottery $L_1 = [\$50, 0.5; \$100, 0.5]$ he attaches to gains \$50 and \$100 a decision weight of only $0.5^2 = 0.25$, so that for him the OPT value of L_1 is "only" $0.5^2 \times 50 + 0.5^2 \times 100 = 37.5$. In contrast, the probability $p = 1$ of obtaining \$40 with certainty is not distorted, so that the OPT value of $L_2 = [\$40,1]$ is $1^2 \times 40 = 40$. Therefore, according to OPT, this decision maker prefers the stochastically dominated lottery L_2 to L_1.

7.2 Cumulative Prospect Theory

In order to avoid violations of stochastic dominance while maintaining the idea that decision makers may substitute decision weights for probabilities, Quiggin (1982) advanced a theory called rank dependent utility theory. This theory features a "traditional" utility function $u(x)$ defined over final states of wealth and presents the novel idea that the weight a decision maker attaches to an outcome depends not only on its probability but also on its rank in the ordering of outcomes from the worst to the best.

In 1992, Kahneman and Tversky advanced a modified version of OPT called cumulative prospect theory (CPT), which supersedes the problem of violations of stochastic dominance allowed by OPT. Cumulative prospect theory combines elements from OPT, such as a value function $v(y)$ which distinguishes gains from losses with respect to a reference point, and elements from rank dependent utility theory, such as rank-dependent probability weighting.

7.2.1 Ranks and Cumulative Probabilities

In CPT, the outcomes of a lottery are reordered from the worst (y_1) to the best (y_N), so that each outcome has its own "rank" in this ordering. In particular, it will be assumed that outcomes from y_1 to y_k are losses, and outcomes from y_{k+1} to y_N are gains with respect to some reference point. Correspondingly, probabilities from p_1 to p_k are the probabilities of losses, and probabilities from p_{k+1} to p_N are the probabilities of gains.

For gains, the probability sum $(p_i + p_{i+1} + p_{i+2} + \ldots + p_N)$, called "cumulative probability," is the probability of gaining y_i or more than y_i. Analogously, for losses the cumulative probability $(p_1 + p_2 + p_3 + \ldots + p_i)$ is the probability of losing y_i or more than y_i.

Consider, for example, lottery $[-\$100,0.1; -\$50,0.2; \$20,0.3; \$80,0.4]$. Here, the ranking of outcomes from the worst to the best is $y_1 = -\$100$, $y_2 = -\$50$, $y_3 = \$20$, and $y_4 = \$80$. The cumulative probability of, for instance, gaining at least \$20 is given by the probability of gaining \$20 plus the probability of gaining \$80, that is, $0.3 + 0.4 = 0.7$.

Cumulative probabilities are rank-dependent, in the sense that if for some reason the rank of an outcome changes, the cumulative probability attached to it also changes. Consider, for example, a modification of the previous lottery such as $[-\$100,0.1; \$20,0.3; \$50,0.2; \$80,0.4]$. Here, the probability $p = 0.2$ of

losing $50 has been transformed into an equal probability $p = 0.2$ of gaining
$50, while the other outcomes and their probabilities have not changed. The
probability of gaining $20 has remained $p = 0.3$, but the rank of this outcome
has changed, passing from second-best to third-best. Accordingly, the cumulative probability of gaining at least $20 has changed too, and it is now given by
$0.3 + 0.2 + 0.4 = 0.9$.

7.2.2 Weighting Cumulative Probabilities

In CPT, the weighting function applies to cumulative probabilities, which
are rank-dependent, rather than single probabilities, which are not rank-
dependent. Moreover, in CPT the weighting function for gains, indicated as
$w^+(p)$, is different from the weighting function for losses, indicated as
$w^-(p)$. The idea is that, just as decision makers attach different subjective
values $v(y)$ to gains and losses, they may also attach different weights to
gains and losses.

More precisely, $w^+(p_i + \ldots + p_N)$ expresses the weight that the decision
maker attaches to the cumulative probability of gaining at least y_i, while
$w^-(p_1 + \ldots + p_i)$ expresses the weight that the decision maker assigns to the
cumulative probability of losing y_i or more than y_i. To continue our example
with lottery $[-\$100, 0.1; -\$50, 0.2; \$20, 0.3; \$80, 0.4]$, and assuming that
$w^+(p) = p^2$, the weight that the decision maker attaches to the probability of
gaining at least $20 is $(0.3 + 0.4)^2 = 0.49$.

7.2.3 Decision weights in CPT

As discussed in Section 7.1.3, in OPT the decision weight that a decision maker
attaches to an outcome y_i is given, for both gains and losses, by $w(p_i)$. In CPT,
things are more complicated.

The decision weight attached to a gain y_i is given by $w^+(p_i + \ldots + p_N) -
w^+(p_{i+1} + \ldots + p_N)$, that is, by the difference between the weight that the
decision maker attaches to the probability of gaining at least y_i, and the weight
that he attaches to the probability of gaining strictly more than y_i. In particular,
because the probability of gaining strictly more than the maximum gain y_N is
zero, the decision weight attached to y_N is $w^+(p_N)$.

For losses, the decision weight attached to a loss y_i is equal to
$w^-(p_1 + \ldots + p_i) - w^-(p_1 + \ldots + p_{i-1})$, that is, to the difference between
the weight that the decision maker attaches to the probability of losing y_i or
more than y_i and the weight he attaches to the probability of losing strictly more
than y_i. Because the probability of losing strictly more than the maximum
possible loss y_1 is zero, the decision weight attached to y_1 is $w^-(p_1)$.

Decision weighting as modeled in CPT can be shown to exclude violations of stochastic dominance and thus overcomes one of the main limitations of OPT (see Section 7.1.6). However, CPT decision weighting remains problematic from a normative viewpoint because it still states that the decision maker distorts the objective probabilities he is supposed to know. In our example, the decision maker knows that the objective probabilities of losing $100 and gaining $20 are 0.1 and 0.4, respectively, but attaches decision weights equal to 0.32 and 0.16 to them.

7.2.4 The CPT Formula

Now, according to CPT, the decision maker prefers the lottery associated with the maximum value of the following functional form:

$$\sum_{i=1}^{k} v(y_i) \left[w^-(p_1 + \ldots + p_i) - w^-(p_1 + \ldots + p_{i-1}) \right]$$
$$+ \sum_{i=k+1}^{N} v(y_i) \left[w^+(p_i + \ldots + p_N) - w^+(p_{i+1} + \ldots + p_N) \right],$$

whereby the decision weights attached to y_1 and y_N are, respectively, $w^-(p_1)$ and $w^+(p_N)$. In our example, and assuming that $w^+(p) = p^2$ and $w^-(p) = \sqrt{p}$, and that $v(y) = y$ for both gains and losses, the CPT value of lottery $[-\$100,0.1; -\$50,0.2; \$20,0.3; \$80,0.4]$ is given by

$$-100 \times \sqrt{0.1} - 50 \times \left[\sqrt{0.3} - \sqrt{0.1} \right] + 20 \times \left[0.7^2 - 0.4^2 \right] + 80 \times 0.4^2$$
$$= -23.1.$$

A negative CPT value means that the decision maker will (if he can) refrain from participating in this lottery. Since its expected payoff is equal to $18, and the CPT value of $18 is $18 \times 1^2 = 18$, this decision maker prefers $18 for sure to playing the lottery, so he is actuarially risk-averse.

Note that if $w^+(p) = w^-(p) = p$, that is, if objective probabilities are not distorted, if $v(y)$ is the same for gains and losses and $r = 0$, the CPT formula coincides with the EU formula. Accordingly, CPT can also be seen as a generalization of EU, although different from the generalization offered by original prospect theory. In fact, while OPT can account for choice patterns that violate stochastic dominance, CPT rules out such violations.

In the paper where they advance CPT, Tversky and Kahneman (1992) did not offer a preference-based version of the theory, which was, however, provided by Wakker and Tversky (1993). As in von Neumann and Morgenstern's EU, in the preference-based version of CPT the primary element of the analysis is a preference relation $\succcurlyeq$ between lotteries. Like the preference relation represented by the EU formula, the preference relation represented by the CPT formula is also assumed to be complete and transitive. Other properties of the former relation, and notably the Independence Axiom, are weakened or dropped.

CPT can also be extended to analyze situations of decision-making under uncertainty where the objective probabilities of events are not available and decision makers have beliefs about the likelihood of events (see Wakker 2010).

7.2.5 Allais, Ellsberg, and Risk Attitudes in CPT

Like prospect theory, CPT has more free variables than EU, namely four: $v(y)$, r, $w^+(p)$, and $w^-(p)$. This feature allows CPT to accommodate choice patterns violating EU, such as choice patterns à la Allais, or, when CPT is extended to situations of decision-making under uncertainty, choice patterns à la Ellsberg (see, e.g., Wakker 2010).

Again as in the case of OPT, the multiplicity of free variables also allows CPT to express different psychological factors that may affect the decision maker's preferences between lotteries. In particular, risk attitudes can be accounted for not only by the form of the value function $v(y)$ but also by the form of the weighting functions $w^+(p)$ and $w^-(p)$.

For instance, a decision maker whose weighting functions are such that (1) he overrates the probabilities of worse outcomes, that is, of outcomes that occupy lower ranks in the ordering $y_1, \ldots, y_N$, and (2) he underrates the probabilities of better outcomes that occupy higher ranks in that ordering can be considered a "pessimistic" decision maker, who, other conditions been equal, will tend to be risk-averse.

This is the case of the decision maker of our numerical example, who attaches a decision weight of 0.32 to the worst outcome (losing $100), which in fact has a probability of 0.1, and a decision weight of 0.16 to the best outcome (gaining $80), which has a probability of 0.4. As mentioned, this decision maker is risk-averse, although his value function $v(y) = y$ is linear, so that the diminishing marginal value of money is ruled out, and $v(y)$ is equal for both gains and losses, so that loss aversion is excluded. Therefore, his risk aversion draws entirely from the form of his weighting functions $w^+(p)$ and $w^-(p)$.

7.2.6 Criticisms of CPT

A first criticism of CPT is similar to the one mentioned with reference to OPT: CPT has too many free variables that can be arbitrarily specified so that, ex post, it can rationalize almost any observed choice pattern (see, e.g., Berg & Gigerenzer 2010).

A second and more recent criticism, advanced by Bernheim and Sprenger (2020), is that experimental evidence does not support the rank-dependent probability weighting postulated by CPT but rather a rank-independent probability weighting like that assumed by original prospect theory. In particular, Bernheim and Sprenger put forward a modified version of OPT, in which probability weights are rank-independent but decision makers are "averse to complexity," in the sense that they "prefer lotteries with fewer outcomes because they are easier to understand" (1367). This type of complexity aversion is absent from OPT, and for Bernheim and Sprenger it can account for a series of experimental data that cannot be accommodated by OPT.

Supporters of CPT such as Abdellaoui et al. (2020) have criticized the validity of Bernheim and Sprenger's experimental evidence against rank-dependent probability weighting and CPT. Bernheim and coauthors (Bernheim, Royer, & Sprenger 2022) have pushed back against these criticisms and offered further experimental evidence supporting the robustness of their experimental findings.

Clearly, the debate on prospect theory and its variants, as well as, more generally, on theories of decision-making that go beyond EU, remains an open one.

7.3 The As-If Interpretation of Prospect Theory

Proponents of decision models alternative to EU have often criticized the as-if approach to economic modeling that Friedman, Savage, and other mainstream economists have used to defend EU against the accusation of lack of psychological realism (see Section 5.8). According to scholars such as Thaler (1980, 2016), Rabin (1998), and Camerer and Loewenstein (2004), decision models not only should be able to account for the observable choices that individuals make but should also figure out correctly the underlying psychological processes that generate those choices. These scholars also claim that their decision models fulfil this requirement and that this is the reason why they account for choice behavior better than EU.

In Moscati (in press), I argue that, contrary to what their proponents claim, the models alternative to EU currently used in decision theory are also best understood as as-if models. The main argument in support of this claim is that the psychological mechanisms posited by non-EU models are cognitively as demanding as those posited by EU itself and therefore cannot be implemented by actual decision makers. Here, I briefly consider the case of OPT and CPT.

If we consider the OPT formula $\sum v(y_i)w(p_i)$ and the CPT formula $\sum v(y_i)[w^-(p_1 + \ldots + p_i) - w^-(p_1 + \ldots + p_{i-1})] + \sum v(y_i)[w^+(p_i + \ldots + p_N) - w^+(p_{i+1} + \ldots + p_N)]$, they are as complicated as, if not more complicated than, the EU formula $\sum u(x_i)p_i$. Therefore, as it is implausible that decision makers actually calculate and compare the EU values of lotteries, so it is implausible that they calculate and compare their OPT and CPT values.

If we move to the preference-based mechanism featured in OPT and CPT, it still relies on the assumption that decision makers harbor in their minds complete, transitive, and stable preferences between risky options. As discussed in Section 5.4, however, it is doubtful that this is the case. Accordingly, it is implausible to consider the risk preferences featured in OPT/CPT and the preference-based decision mechanism relying on them as psychological entities and processes actually existing and operating in the decision maker's mind. Rather, just like the risk preferences and the preference-based mechanism featured in EU, they are best understood as theoretical constructs through which decision theorists describe or predict the behavior of decision makers.

Finally, the fact that OPT and CPT account for observed choice behaviors better than EU does not need to draw from the alleged circumstance that these models capture the psychological processes generating choice behavior better than EU. As discussed in Sections 7.1.6 and 7.2.6, the enhanced descriptive power of OPT and CPT may just be a consequence of the mathematical fact that they feature more free parameters than EU.

8 A Very Short Conclusion

In this Element, I have reviewed EU and its evolution from Bernoulli to Savage, with forays into the pre-history of the theory, namely the expected-payoff hypothesis of Pascal, Fermat, and Huygens, as well as into its "post-history," namely Kahneman and Tversky's prospect theory. I have also discussed the main methodological issues that have accompanied the history of EU and offered my view on them.

One main take-home message, I submit, is that the simplicity of the formula $\sum u(x_i)p(E_i)$ associated with EU is only apparent and that EU is in fact a complicated and multifaceted theoretical object, the interpretation and use of which is often tricky. I hope that this Element may help all scholars interested in EU to understand it better and deal confidently with its subtleties.

References

Abdellaoui, M., P. Klibanoff, and L. Placido. 2015. "Ambiguity and Compound Risk Attitudes: An Experiment." *Management Science* 61: 1306–1322.

Abdellaoui, M., C. Li, P. P. Wakker, and G. Wu. 2020. "A Defense of Prospect Theory in Bernheim & Sprenger's Experiment." Unpublished working paper. https://personal.eur.nl/wakker/pdf/wak.bernh.r.sp.pdf.

Allais, M. 1953. "Le comportement de l'homme rationnel devant le risque." *Econometrica* 21: 503–546.

Andersen, S., G. Harrison, M. Lau, and E. Rutström. 2008. "Lost in State Space: Are Preferences Stable?" *International Economic Review* 49: 1091–1112.

Anscombe, F. and R. Aumann. 1963. "A Definition of Subjective Probability." *Annals of Mathematical Statistics* 34: 199–205.

Aumann, R. 1962. "Utility Theory without the Completeness Axiom." *Econometrica* 30: 445–462.

Aumann, R. [1971] 2000. "Letter from Robert Aumann to Leonard Savage and Letter from Leonard Savage to Robert Aumann." In R. Aumann, *Collected Papers*, Vol. 2, 305–310.

Baccelli, J. 2017. "Do Bets Reveal Beliefs?" *Synthese* 194: 3393–3419.

Baccelli, J. 2021. "The Problem of State-Dependent Utility: A Reappraisal." *British Journal for the Philosophy of Science* 72: 617–634.

Baccelli, J. and P. Mongin. 2022. "Can Redescriptions of Outcomes Salvage the Axioms of Decision Theory?" *Philosophical Studies* 179: 1621–1648.

Barseghyan, L., J. Prince, and J. C. Teitelbaum. 2011. "Are Risk Preferences Stable across Contexts? Evidence from Insurance Data." *American Economic Review* 101: 591–631.

Beauchamp, J. P., D. J. Benjamin, D. I. Laibson, and C. F. Chabris. 2020. "Measuring and Controlling for the Compromise Effect When Estimating Risk Preference Parameters." *Experimental Economics* 23: 1069–1099.

Berg, N. and G. Gigerenzer. 2010. "As-If Behavioral Economics: Neoclassical Economics in Disguise?" *History of Economic Ideas* 18: 133–165.

Bernheim, B. D., R. Royer, and C. Sprenger. 2022. "Robustness of Rank Independence in Risky Choice." *American Economic Review, Papers and Proceedings* 112: 415–420.

Bernheim, B. D. and C. Sprenger. 2020. "On the Empirical Validity of Cumulative Prospect Theory." *Econometrica* 88: 1363–1409.

Bernoulli, D. [1738] 1954. "Exposition of a New Theory on the Measurement of Risk." *Econometrica* 22: 23–36.

Bernoulli, D. [1738] 1982. *Specimen theoriae novae de mensura sortis.* In D. Speiser, ed., *Die Werke von Daniel Bernoulli,* Vol. 2, 223–234. Basel: Birkhäuser.

Bernoulli, J. [1713] 2006. *The Art of Conjecturing.* Baltimore, MD: Johns Hopkins University Press.

Bernoulli, N. [1709] 1975. *De usu artis conjectandi in iure.* In B. L. van der Waerden, ed., *Die Werke von Jakob Bernoulli,* Vol. 3, 287–326. Basel: Birkhäuser.

Binmore, K. 2009. *Rational Decisions.* Princeton, NJ: Princeton University Press.

Bordalo, P., N. Gennaioli, and A. Shleifer. 2022. "Salience." *Annual Review of Economics* 14, 521–544.

Bradley, R. 2017. *Decision Theory with a Human Face.* Cambridge: Cambridge University Press.

Brandstätter, E., G. Gigerenzer, and R. Hertwig. 2006. "The Priority Heuristic." *Psychological Review* 113: 409–432.

Broome, J. 1990. "Bolker–Jeffrey Expected Utility Theory and Axiomatic Utilitarianism." *Review of Economic Studies* 57: 477–502.

Buchak, L. 2013. *Risk and Rationality.* Oxford: Oxford University Press.

Cairnes, J. E. 1872. "New Theories in Political Economy." *Fortnightly Review* 9: 71–76.

Camerer, C. F. and G. Loewenstein. 2004. "Behavioral Economics." In C. F. Camerer, G. Loewenstein, and M. Rabin, eds., *Advances in Behavioral Economics,* 3–51. Princeton, NJ: Princeton University Press.

Chateauneuf, A. 1985. "On the Existence of a Probability Measure Compatible with a Total Preorder on a Boolean Algebra." *Journal of Mathematical Economics* 14: 43–52.

Davidson, D., J. C. C. McKinsey, and P. Suppes. 1955. "Outlines of a Formal Theory of Value, I." *Philosophy of Science* 22: 140–160.

de Finetti, B. [1937] 1980. "Foresight: Its Logical Flaws, Its Subjective Sources." In H. E. Kyburg and H. E. Smokler, eds., *Studies in Subjective Probability,* 93–158. New York: Wiley.

Einav, L., A. Finkelstein, I. Pascu, and M. R. Cullen. 2012. "How General Are Risk Preferences?" *American Economic Review* 102: 2606–2638.

Ellsberg, D. 1961. "Risk, Ambiguity, and the Savage Axioms." *Quarterly Journal of Economics* 75: 643–669.

Fishburn, P. C. 1978. "On Handa's 'New Theory of Cardinal Utility' and the Maximization of Expected Return." *Journal of Political Economy* 86: 321–324.

Friedman, M. 1953. "The Methodology of Positive Economics." In M. Friedman, *Essays in Positive Economics*, 3–43. Chicago, IL: University of Chicago Press.

Friedman, M. and L. J. Savage. 1948. "The Utility Analysis of Choices Involving Risk." *Journal of Political Economy* 56: 279–304.

Friedman, M. and L. J. Savage. 1952. "The Expected-Utility Hypothesis and the Measurability of Utility." *Journal of Political Economy* 60: 463–474.

Gilboa, I. 2009. *Theory of Decision under Uncertainty*. Cambridge: Cambridge University Press.

Gilboa, I. and M. Marinacci. 2013. "Ambiguity and the Bayesian Paradigm." In D. Acemoglu, M. Arellano, and E. Dekel, eds., *Advances in Economics and Econometrics*, Vol. 1, 179–242. New York: Cambridge University Press.

Gilboa, I., A. Postlewaite, and D. Schmeidler. 2008. "Probability and Uncertainty in Economic Modeling." *Journal of Economic Perspectives* 22: 173–188.

Gilboa, I., A. Postlewaite, and D. Schmeidler. 2012. "Rationality of Belief or: Why Savage's Axioms Are Neither Necessary Nor Sufficient for Rationality." *Synthese* 187: 11–31.

Gilboa, I., A. Postlewaite, and D. Schmeidler. 2021. "The Complexity of the Consumer Problem." *Research in Economics* 75: 96–103.

Gustafsson, J. E. 2022. *Money-Pump Arguments*. Cambridge: Cambridge University Press.

Hacking, I. 1975. *The Emergence of Probability*. Cambridge: Cambridge University Press.

Handa, J. 1977. "Risk, Probabilities, and a New Theory of Cardinal Utility." *Journal of Political Economy* 85: 97–122.

Harrison, G. W., J. Martínez-Correa, and J. T. Swarthout. 2015. "Reduction of Compound Lotteries with Objective Probabilities." *Journal of Economic Behavior & Organization* 119: 32–55.

Herne, K. 1999. "The Effects of Decoy Gambles on Individual Choice." *Experimental Economics* 2: 31–40.

Hicks, J. R. 1931. "The Theory of Uncertainty and Profit." *Economica* 32: 170–189.

Hicks, J. R. 1934. "The Application of Mathematical Methods to the Theory of Risk." *Econometrica* 2: 194–195.

Hicks, J. R. 1939. *Value and Capital*. Oxford: Clarendon Press.

Huber, J., J. W. Payne, and C. Puto. 1982. "Adding Asymmetrically Dominated Alternatives." *Journal of Consumer Research* 9: 90–98.

Huygens, C. [1657] 1920. *De ratiociniis in ludo aleae*. In *Œuvres complètes de Christiaan Huygens*, vol. 14, 50–175. La Haye: Nijhoff.

Jeffrey, R. C. [1965] 1990. *The Logic of Decision.* Chicago, IL: University of Chicago Press.

Jevons, W. S. 1871. *The Theory of Political Economy.* London: Macmillan.

Kahneman, D. and A. Tversky. 1979. "Prospect Theory: An Analysis of Decision under Risk." *Econometrica* 47: 263–292.

Karni, E. 1996. "Probabilities and Beliefs." *Journal of Risk and Uncertainty* 13: 249–262.

Karni, E. 2008. "State-Dependent Utility." In P. Anand, P. Pattanaik, and C. Puppe, eds., *The Handbook of Rational and Social Choice*, 223–238. Oxford: Oxford University Press.

Keynes, J. M. 1921. *A Treatise on Probability.* London: Macmillan.

Knight, F. H. 1921. *Risk, Uncertainty, and Profit.* Boston, MA: Houghton Mifflin.

Kolmogorov, A. 1933. *Grundbegriffe der Wahrscheinlichkeitsrechnung.* Berlin: Springer.

Koopman, B. O. 1940. "The Axioms and Algebra of Intuitive Probability." *Annals of Mathematics* 41: 269–262.

Kraft, H. C., W. J. Pratt, and A. Seidenberg. 1959. "Intuitive Probability on Finite Sets." *Annals of Mathematical Statistics* 30: 408–419.

Kreps, D. 1988. *Notes on the Theory of Choice.* Boulder, CO: Westview Press.

Laplace, P.-S. 1812. *Théorie analytique des probabilités.* Paris: Courcier.

Leonard, R. 1995. "From Parlor Games to Social Science." *Journal of Economic Literature* 33: 730–761.

Lewis, D. 1974. "Radical Interpretation." *Synthese* 23: 331–344.

Lewis, D. [1980] 1987. "A Subjectivist's Guide to Objective Chance." In D. Lewis, *Philosophical Papers*, Vol. 2, 83–113. New York: Oxford University Press.

Lichtenstein, S. and P. Slovic. 1971. "Reversals of Preference between Bids and Choices in Gambling Decisions." *Journal of Experimental Psychology* 89: 46–55.

Lichtenstein, S. and P. Slovic, eds. 2006. *The Construction of Preference.* New York: Cambridge University Press.

Lipman, B. L. and W. Pesendorfer. 2013. "Temptation." In D. Acemoglu, M. Arellano, and E. Dekel, eds., *Advances in Economics and Econometrics*, 243–288. New York: Cambridge University Press.

Luce, R. D. and H. Raiffa. 1957. *Games and Decisions.* New York: Wiley.

Marschak, J. 1950. "Rational Behavior, Uncertain Prospects, and Measurable Utility." *Econometrica* 18: 111–141.

Marshall, A. 1890. *Principles of Economics.* London: Macmillan.

Mas-Colell, A., M. D. Whinston, and J. R. Green. 1995. *Microeconomic Theory.* New York: Oxford University Press.

Mata, R. and F. Nagel. 2023. "On an Unknown Early Version of Daniel Bernoulli's *Specimen theoriae novae de mensura sortis*." Unpublished working paper. https://doi.org/10.31234/osf.io/49f6s.

Menger, C. [1871] 1981. *Principles of Economics*. New York: New York University Press.

Montesano, A. 1985. "The Ordinal Utility under Uncertainty and the Measure of Risk Aversion in Terms of Preferences." *Theory and Decision* 18: 73–85.

Moscati, I. 2007. "History of Consumer Demand Theory 1871–1971." *European Journal of the History of Economic Thought* 14: 119–156.

Moscati, I. 2013. "How Cardinal Utility Entered Economic Analysis: 1909–1944." *European Journal of the History of Economic Thought* 20: 906–939.

Moscati, I. 2016. "How Economists Came to Accept Expected Utility Theory: The Case of Samuelson and Savage." *Journal of Economic Perspectives* 30: 219–236.

Moscati, I. 2018. *Measuring Utility: From the Marginal Revolution to Behavioral Economics*. New York: Oxford University Press.

Moscati, I. In press "Behavioural and Heuristic Models Are As-If Models Too – And That's Ok." *Economics and Philosophy*. http://doi:10.1017 /S0266267123000093.

Mosteller, F. and P. Nogee. 1951. "An Experimental Measurement of Utility." *Journal of Political Economy* 59: 371–404.

Nuerk, H.-C., K. Moeller, and K. Willmes. 2015. "Multi-Digit Number Processing." In R. C. Kadosh and A. Dowker, eds., *The Oxford Handbook of Numerical Cognition*, 106–139. Oxford: Oxford University Press.

O'Donoghue, T. and J. Somerville. 2018. "Modeling Risk Aversion in Economics." *Journal of Economic Perspectives* 32: 91–114.

Okasha, S. 2016. "On the Interpretation of Decision Theory." *Economics and Philosophy* 32: 409–433.

Pareto, V. 1896. *Cours d'économie politique*, Vol. 1. Lausanne: Rouge.

Pareto, V. [1906/9] 2014. *Manual of Political Economy*, ed. by A. Montesano, A. Zanni, L. Bruni, J. S. Chipman, and M. McLure. New York: Oxford University Press.

Peterson, M. 2004. "From Outcomes to Acts: A Non-Standard Axiomatization of the Expected Utility Principle." *Journal of Philosophical Logic* 33: 361–378.

Peterson, M. 2017. *An Introduction to Decision Theory*. New York: Cambridge University Press.

Prelec, D. 1998. "The Probability Weighting Function." *Econometrica* 66: 497–527.

Quiggin, J. 1982. "A Theory of Anticipated Utility." *Journal of Economic Behavior and Organization* 3: 323–343.

Rabin, M. 1998. "Psychology and Economics." *Journal of Economic Literature* 36: 11–46.

Ramsey, F. P. [1926] 1931. "Truth and Probability." In R. B. Braithwaite, ed., *Foundations of Mathematics and Other Logical Essays*, 156–198. London: Kegan Paul.

Rubinstein, A. 1988. "Similarity and Decision-Making under Risk." *Journal of Economic Theory* 46: 145–153.

Samuelson, P. A. 1947. *Foundations of Economic Analysis*. Cambridge, MA: Harvard University Press.

Samuelson, P. A. 1950. "Probability and the Attempts to Measure Utility." *Economic Review* 1: 167–173.

Samuelson, P. A. 1952. "Probability, Utility, and the Independence Axiom." *Econometrica* 20: 670–678.

Savage, L. J. [1954] 1972. *The Foundations of Statistics*. New York: Dover.

Schmoller, G. 1883. "Zur Methodologie der Staats und Sozialwissenschaften." *Jahrbuch für Gesetzgebung, Verwaltung und Volkswirtschaft im deutschen Reich* 8: 974–994.

Schoemaker, P. J. H. 1982. "The Expected Utility Model: Its Variants, Purposes, Evidence and Limitations." *Journal of Economic Literature* 20: 529–563.

Segal, U. 1992. "The Independence Axiom versus the Reduction Axiom." In W. Edwards, ed., *Utility Theories: Measurements and Applications*, 165–183. Boston, MA: Kluwer.

Shafer, G. 1981. "Constructive Probability." *Synthese* 48: 1–60.

Simonson, I. 1989. "Choice Based on Reasons: The Case of Attraction and Compromise Effects." *Journal of Consumer Research* 16: 158–174.

Spiess, O. 1975. "Zur Vorgeschichte des Petersburger Problems." In B. L. van der Waerden, ed., *Die Werke von Jakob Bernoulli*, Vol. 3, 557–567. Basel: Birkhäuser.

Starmer, C. 2000. "Developments in Non-expected Utility Theory." *Journal of Economic Literature* 38: 332–382.

Steele, K. and H. Orri Stefánsson. 2020. "Decision Theory." In E. N. Zalta, ed., *Stanford Encyclopedia of Philosophy* (Winter 2020 ed.). https://plato.stanford.edu/archives/win2020/entries/decision-theory/.

Thaler, R. 1980. "Toward a Positive Theory of Consumer Choice." *Journal of Economic Behavior & Organization* 1: 39–60.

Thaler, R. 2016. "Behavioral Economics." *American Economic Review* 106: 1577–1600.

Tversky, A. 1969. "Intransitivity of Preferences." *Psychological Review* 76: 31–48.

Tversky, A. and D. Kahneman. 1992. "Advances in Prospect Theory: Cumulative Representation of Uncertainty." *Journal of Risk and Uncertainty* 5: 297–323.

von Neumann, J. and O. Morgenstern. [1944] 1953. *Theory of Games and Economic Behavior*. Princeton, NJ: Princeton University Press.

Wakker P. P. 2010. *Prospect Theory*. Cambridge: Cambridge University Press.

Wakker, P. P. and A. Tversky. 1993. "An Axiomatization of Cumulative Prospect Theory." *Journal of Risk and Uncertainty* 7: 147–175.

Walras, L. [1874] 1954. *Elements of Pure Economics*. London: Allen and Unwin.

Zeisberger, S., D. Vrecko, and T. Langer. 2012. "Measuring the Time Stability of Prospect Theory Preferences." *Theory and Decision* 72: 359–386.

Zynda, L. 2000. "Representation Theorems and Realism about Degrees of Belief." *Philosophy of Science* 67: 45–69.

Acknowledgments

I am grateful to two anonymous referees for insightful and precise comments and to Pietro Dindo, Conrad Heilmann, Marco Li Calzi, and the participants to a workshop at Erasmus University Rotterdam for helpful comments and discussions. I am also grateful to Martin Peterson, the editor of this Cambridge series, for useful suggestions about the structure of the Element. I wrote some sections while visiting the Department of Economics at Ca' Foscari University of Venice and the Erasmus Institute for Philosophy and Economics at Erasmus University Rotterdam; I am grateful to these institutions for their kind hospitality. Parts of this Element draw on related work of mine, namely the monograph *Measuring Utility: From the Marginal Revolution to Behavioral Economics* (Oxford University Press, 2018) and the articles "How Economists Came to Accept Expected Utility Theory: The Case of Samuelson and Savage," *Journal of Economic Perspectives* 30: 219–236 (2016), and "Behavioural and Heuristic Models Are As-if Models Too – And That's Ok," *Economics and Philosophy* (in press).

I dedicate this work to the "Old Masters" who introduced me and several other students to the beauties and subtleties of decision theory: Erio Castagnoli, Marco Dardi, Philippe Mongin, and Aldo Montesano.

Cambridge Elements ☰

Decision Theory and Philosophy

Martin Peterson
Texas A&M University

Martin Peterson is Professor of Philosophy and Sue and Harry E. Bovay Professor of the History and Ethics of Professional Engineering at Texas A&M University. He is the author of four books and one edited collection, as well as many articles on decision theory, ethics and philosophy of science.

About the Series

This Cambridge Elements series offers an extensive overview of decision theory in its many and varied forms. Distinguished authors provide an up-to-date summary of the results of current research in their fields and give their own take on what they believe are the most significant debates influencing research, drawing original conclusions.

Cambridge Elements ≡

Decision Theory and Philosophy